T0370130

AMISH VOICES

VOLUME 2

"In this wonderful and engaging compilation of excerpts from the Amish publication *Family Life*, Brad Igou takes us on a journey from the sacrifices and martyrdom of the Amish past to the intricacies of the Amish present and, finally, to the challenges of the Amish future. In every chapter, Igou gifts us with an inside look at Amish life in Amish words."

—**KAREN M. JOHNSON-WEINER**, distinguished service professor emerita in the Anthropology Department at SUNY Potsdam and author of *All about the Amish* and *The Lives of Amish Women*

"Brad Igou lets us hear genuine Amish voices as they discuss the things that matter most to them. Selected from a quarter century of Amish publication, this collection of writings allows us to listen in on conversations about child-rearing, occupational change, concerns about cell phone use, and much more. A wonderful source for understanding Amish life."

—**STEVEN M. NOLT**, interim director and senior scholar at the Young Center for Anabaptist and Pietist Studies at Elizabethtown College and coauthor of *Amish Grace: How Forgiveness Transcended Tragedy*

"Why do the Amish live the way they do? What do they care about and why? What challenges do they face in living up to their ideals? Learn about the Amish from the Amish themselves in this enlightening compilation of writing spanning faith and church, marriage, raising children, work, the world's temptations, community, and more."

—**ERIK WESNER**, founder of the Amish America website and YouTube channel

"Brad Igou organized over twenty-five years of Amish readers' submissions to *Family Life* magazine, a monthly publication found in almost every Amish home. Compelling and easy to read, *Amish Voices, Volume 2* invites readers into Amish culture via letters written with simple eloquence. Witty and poignant, plainspoken and nuanced, this book presents Amish insights on the joy of children, becoming a better parent, the deep loss of a spouse, the privilege of aging, work, family, and community life. Easy to read and hard to put down!"

—**JUDY STAVISKY,** author of *In Plain View: The Daily Lives of Amish Women*

"My only complaint about Brad Igou's previous collection of Amish voices was that I wanted to hear more. And now I can. This volume will take its place beside the previous one on my easy-to-reach, frequently accessed shelf."

—**DAVID WEAVER-ZERCHER,** professor of American religious history at Messiah University

"Brad Igou has created a beautiful collection of stories that come directly from the Amish heart. This book will capture *your* heart as it paints a vivid and authentic portrait of the Amish men and women who live their lives with humble obedience to God's will as interpreted by a disciplined community of faith. *Amish Voices, Volume 2* will fill you with a peace that seems to be lacking in this modern world where we reside today."

—**SUSAN HOUGELMAN,** author of *Inside the Simple Life: Finding Inspiration among the Amish*

AMISH VOICES

VOLUME 2
In Their Own Words, 1993–2020

BRAD IGOU, *compiler*

HERALD
P R E S S

Harrisonburg, Virginia

Herald Press
PO Box 866, Harrisonburg, Virginia 22803
www.HeraldPress.com

Library of Congress Cataloging-in-Publication Data
Names: Igou, Brad, 1951- editor..
Title: Amish voices. Volume 2, In their own words, 1993-2020 / Brad Igou, compiler.
Other titles: Family life (Aylmer, Ont.)
Description: Harrisonburg : Herald Press, 2023. | Edited excerpts from articles
   published in a monthly magazine called Family Life, written and published by
   Amish people.
Identifiers: LCCN 2022037375 (print) | LCCN 2022037376 (ebook) | ISBN
   9781513811871 (paperback) | ISBN 9781513811888 (hardcover) | ISBN
   9781513811895 (ebook)
Subjects: LCSH: Amish--Social life and customs. | Mennonite Church. | BISAC:
   RELIGION / Christianity / Amish | TRAVEL / Special Interest / Religious
Classification: LCC BX8129.A5 A4322 2023 (print) | LCC BX8129.A5 (ebook)
   | DDC 289.7/3--dc23/eng/20221025
LC record available at https://lccn.loc.gov/2022037375
LC ebook record available at https://lccn.loc.gov/2022037376

Unless otherwise noted, scripture is adapted from the *King James Version* of the
Holy Bible.

These excerpts from *Family Life* magazine, Pathway Publishers, 10380 Carter Road,
Aylmer, ON N5H 2R3, Canada, are gratefully used and adapted by permission.

AMISH VOICES, VOLUME 2
© 2023 by Herald Press, Harrisonburg, Virginia 22803. 800-245-7894.
   All rights reserved.
Library of Congress Control Number: 2022037375
International Standard Book Number: 978-1-5138-1187-1 (paperback);
   978-1-5138-1188-8 (hardcover); 978-1-5138-1189-5 (ebook)

Printed in United States of America
Cover photo by Jeremy Madea
Design by Merrill Miller

27 26 25 24 23   10 9 8 7 6 5 4 3 2 1

For my parents, Abner, and Joseph

Selections from the first twenty-five years of
Family Life magazine can be found in the first volume
of this two-volume collection:

Amish Voices: A Collection of Amish Writings,
compiled by Brad Igou

Contents

Foreword

HUNDREDS, IF NOT THOUSANDS, of Amish-themed books —most produced in the last twenty-five years—populate the online listings of Amazon and other booksellers. Among this sea of books, the one in your hand stands apart. Unlike most books about the Amish, this one is filled with a multitude of Amish writers—mothers and fathers, farmers and church leaders, who speak their minds and share their opinions about their faith and community.

The writers in volume 2 of *Amish Voices* invite us to sit around an Amish table and listen as Amish people speak about their deepest cares and concerns. This table conversation is more satisfying, more authentically Amish, than the secondhand *interpretations* of Amish life provided by outside scholars, tourist writers, and the so-called bonnet novelists.

The 174 vignettes, situated in the roughly twenty-five years between 1993 and 2020, range from traditional opinions about church, family, and work to more controversial ones on voting, government, and smartphones—to name a few.

In *Amish Voices: In Their Own Words*, ordinary people write in everyday language about the things that matter most to them. We hear about mice, soup, sin, roosters, hemlines, abuse, brain teasers, and Amish worries about their plight in the pendulum of public opinion. These mini-essays are full of joy, humor, and a deep yearning to know God's heart and practice the ways of Jesus.

Amish life is not homogeneous. Communities and individuals do not conform to the mold of a single old-fashioned cultural cookie cutter. Some forty groups of Amish people living in thirty-two different US states and four Canadian provinces produce an abundance of diversity.

Except for a few ultra-conservative groups that consider *Family Life* too progressive, the magazine's writers and readers reflect mainstream Amish life. Its numerous writers, scattered across many geographical areas and groups, represent a diversity of Amish views. They hold one thing in common: their love and commitment to the church, even though they don't always agree on how to fortify it.

Unable to include all the essays written over the twenty-five-year period, compiler Brad Igou had to make choices. He was not making an argument, not trying to prove a point, nor even confirming a hypothesis. Igou sought a balance of voices: the firm and soft, the young and old, the traditional and progressive, the women and men. He aimed to portray a diversity of Amish views to give readers a genuine portal into Amish ideas and perspectives on various topics.

On a personal note, I thoroughly enjoyed the poetry. Amish poetry is not the highbrow kind that makes a reader ponder deep meanings, but the everyday, down-to-earth imagery that reflects the rhyme and rhythm of daily living.

As I read this volume of *Amish Voices*, I could smell the aroma of Amish life, sense the love that authors had for their community, and feel the authentic heartbeat of Amish ways. I listened as writers expressed deep convictions about their faith and church. These were real Amish voices—the unvarnished, unfiltered, full-throated sounds of Amish ways.

These short essays entice us to keep turning the pages, stirring our curiosity about what the next one will bring.

Amish Voices is a delightful read—so delightful that it's hard to put it down.

—Donald B. Kraybill, bestselling author of *The Riddle of Amish Culture* and Senior Fellow Emeritus at Elizabethtown College's Young Center for Anabaptist and Pietist Studies

Preface

THE FIRST JOB I EVER HAD—when I was in college in the early 1970s—was as a tour guide at an Amish attraction where my mother also worked in Lancaster, Pennsylvania. I really did not know much about the Amish at the time, but now I had to learn. I was also trained to do bus tours, and I fell in love with the beautiful farmlands. Over time, I got to know some Amish people and became fascinated as I learned more about them and their way of life. I even changed my major to sociology/anthropology, and managed to spend a semester living and working with an Amish family.

While living with the Amish family, I came upon a monthly magazine called *Family Life*. Written and published by Amish people, in its pages I discovered personal insights not found in academic books. These articles and stories gave me a better idea of what it meant to be Amish, and added to my experience.

Years later, after a stint in the Peace Corps and teaching in Japan, I came home and again started working in the tourism industry. I began to think that the articles in *Family Life* would be valuable for people who sincerely wanted a better understanding of this faith

13

and culture. Quite by chance, I met an Amish man named Abner F. Beiler who had back copies in a library he kept in his home. And so for many years, I would visit once a week after work, writing down and compiling excerpts, until a book of selections from the first twenty-five years of the magazine (1968–92) was published in 1999 as *The Amish in Their Own Words: Amish Writings from 25 Years of* Family Life *Magazine*, followed by a condensed version in 2019 as the first volume of *Amish Voices*. Because of work and other commitments, the idea of doing the next twenty-five years languished for a long time.

In February 2002, I began work on this second volume of *Amish Voices*. I returned to the now relocated Amish library with Abner and started reading once again, beginning with the 1993 issues. But in September, a few months into the new project, Abner passed away. Months went by, and with no one to open the library for me on Wednesday nights, my project stalled. Finally, I wrote a letter to the library requesting permission to borrow the *Family Life* issues, one year at a time. I realized that this would break their policy of not allowing texts to leave the library, but I hoped we could reach an agreement that would allow me to continue the project.

As I had hoped, the men who took care of the library found a solution—one had back issues in his home. At the library one Saturday, Joseph B. Lapp loaned me several years of magazines for "as long as I needed them." And so it was that in March 2003, I again opened a magazine to pick up where I had left off. But my busy work schedule and, at least for a decade, living with my mother in her final years allowed for only very incremental progress. In 2019, I sold my business and retired, but traveling and other interests kept me occupied.

Then the coronavirus pandemic hit in 2020 and I found myself at home all day with a need to get into some kind of routine. It wasn't until I literally stumbled upon that box of back issues from Joe Lapp in my basement that the spark again ignited and I found both the time and the motivation to pick up work on the second book.

Now I began to wonder about getting more back issues. Could Joe Lapp possibly trust me again, after I had basically "lost" those magazines for all those years? With his address label on each magazine, it was easy enough to write a letter saying that I at least wanted to finally return the copies I still had. And I admitted that I could hardly blame him if he did not want to loan me back issues again. I really had no excuse for keeping them for so long.

Joe was most gracious in his response, and when I drove to his home to return what I had borrowed, he willingly gave me a few more years of magazines, and I reaffirmed my commitment to try to work through one issue a day. About this time, I discovered the Dictate function on my laptop, and with this immense help in view of my meager typing skills, I finished in early 2022, having decided to read through the year 2020.

I had over eight hundred pages, which I edited down before submitting the manuscript. An editorial request to bring my book in at under sixty-five thousand words meant a further reduction of about 55 percent, so what you find in these pages is what I felt was the most important material—while regretfully having to leave out some articles I really liked. Article titles are original to those in the magazine, and my own brief introductory remarks, in distinctive type, precede each chapter and some selections. The process of how I sorted and compiled the hundreds of excerpts would take up another page, so I will stop here and just thank all those who helped, encouraged, and supported this project along the way.

—Brad Igou

ONE

What Is *Family Life?*

Note: Parts of this brief introduction are adapted from the first chapter of Amish Voices, *volume 1, my collection of the first twenty-five years (1968–92) of* Family Life.

FAMILY LIFE STARTED IN 1968 as a monthly magazine "dedicated to the promotion of Christian living among the Plain people, with special emphasis on the appreciation of our heritage." At that time, the staff consisted of David Wagler (editor) and Joseph Stoll, David Luthy, Elmo Stoll, and Sarah Weaver (assistant editors). They estimated they would need four thousand subscribers for a forty-page magazine, or five thousand for fifty pages. The annual subscription price was four dollars.

In January 1968, the editors of Pathway Publishing in Aylmer, Ontario, further explained the idea for the magazine by thus answering the question, "What is *Family Life?*":

The family is the heart of the community and the church. Even a nation is made up of families. If there is a strong family life, then the church, the community, and the nation will be likewise. If family life degenerates, then all will suffer.

Family life must be translated into terms of everyday living. What can we do to the community? Do we realize that our everyday work should be a God-given opportunity to serve him? Can we appreciate and make the most of the everyday blessings we receive? Do we stop to enjoy God's creation all around us, and the works of his fingers?

This is the goal of *Family Life*—to be an instrument through which thoughts and ideas can be transmitted.

Over the years, the editors have periodically restated the goal of *Family Life*. In the December 2000 issue, one of the editors summed it up this way when requesting articles from readers:

Our goal is to have *Family Life* reflect the way Christians really live, think, speak, act (and sometimes react!). But it is important for our readers to learn from what they read, and to be encouraged and inspired to a closer walk with God. We encourage writing in simple and clear language, with human interest and strong moral teaching built in rather than tacked on at the end.

In 2009 came this one-sentence summary for readers and writers:

We look forward to hearing from you. Laboring together, we can have a paper that casts light on our paths and strengthens the people of God. —J. E. S.

In January 2010, the Staff Notes column added to a better understanding of how the editors work:

Pathway Publishers was established in 1964 as a nonprofit charitable organization. Those of us who work for Pathway, whether in editing, subscriptions, bookstore, or mopping the floor, are all paid by the hour period. Our hourly wages are set by a board of directors that meets each spring for our annual meeting. —J. S.

By April 1969, *Family Life* was being mailed directly to 8,149 homes and to 113 bookstores for resale in thirty-eight states, four Canadian provinces, and nine other countries, including Germany, Australia, and Japan. As of this writing, the number of subscribers stood at 36,456 (32,767 in the United States and 3,689 in Canada and other countries), according to an article by David Luthy in the October 2020 issue. And in the December 2013 issue I learned that each month they create and distribute two copies in Braille to ten blind readers.

When the editors credit articles submitted by readers, they use what was given to them, anything from full names to initials to unique "signatures." Sometimes readers wish to remain anonymous. I have thus used what the staff supplied after each selection in the book. However, you will see several recurring initials, usually those of one of the Pathway editorial staff during these later years: Joseph Stoll (J. S.), Jonathan E. Stoll (J. E. S.), Christian Stoll (C. S.), David Wagler (D. W.), David Luthy (D. L.), Harvey Miller (H. M.), Elizabeth Wengerd (E. W.), Paul Jantzi (P. J.), Delbert Farmwald (D. F.), and Martha Helmuth (M. H.).

In November 2007, Joseph Stoll described the Staff Notes column as "a last-minute dash of salt and pepper to add to the soup before an issue of *Family Life* goes to press. It is an opportunity for us editors to look at the contents and make a few comments."

As mentioned earlier, readers who send in stories or comments who do not use their initials or actual names often put revealing signatures at the end. Some of my favorites:

Against Bottling Up Steam
A Kentucky Soap Maker

Parents Who Are Still Trying
A Burdened Subscriber
Nosey from Ohio
Content to Be at the Side of the Road
Tired of Being Tired
A Mother Who Has Seen Both Sides
Striving toward the Goal
Needing God's Help Daily
Humbled Again and Again
Longing for a Farm of Our Own
Struggling for a Balance
Broken but Not Defeated
A fellow stumbler
Now wiser, but reaping
A grandfather in Maryland who still likes getting the cows in the
    morning

In various issues, the editors shared insight into the process of making the magazine:

Practically everything that goes into *Family Life* is checked over by a minister, and if it is a doctrinal article or one which is controversial, we like to have several ministers or bishops look it over. After it is published, it goes into nearly every community of Plain folks in the United States and Canada. —July 1972

We [the editors] are all Old Order Amish, and most of our contributors are either Amish or from related "horse and buggy" groups of Plain people. —October 1988

Every issue begins with some pages of letters to the editors, which I always find especially interesting for the varied responses and comments. From time to time, there are differences of opinion over the message or content of a particular article. In the January

1998 issue, Joseph Stoll responded to some writer/reader disagreement about the "facts," saying:

> To those of our readers who are still not convinced, we invite them to present their "circumstantial evidence," but to do so in a reasonable and well-thought-out way that will produce light rather than heat.

He gave similar advice in October 2004 concerning writing letters to the editors for publication:

> If at all possible, end your letter on a positive note. If you criticize, let it be constructive criticism. It is in order to rebuke and correct and challenge a writer's conclusions, but only if you have something better to offer in its place.

The April 2014 issue came with this admonition:

> We don't object to reader response. In fact, we welcome it. Yet we would like to suggest that the letters be brief and to the point, and if necessary, that you set them outside to cool overnight. The old saying is that strong words indicate a weak argument; be advised that we are likely to keep that in mind.

And most recently in May 2019:

> There is one thing we do not want, and that is a personal attack on a certain person or group. We try to not accept any letters that "sow discord among brethren." We prefer not to get involved, or to take sides, in any controversial issue. Not only do we depend on our readers to keep us in line and to correct any errors, we also rely on our readership to help us out when there are questions we cannot answer.

Family Life features many articles on interpretations of the Scriptures. In this compilation, I tried to limit and condense "theological" discussions (risky, I know), and I attempt to give only an idea of Amish interpretations of the Bible and how teachings are applied to their lives. Articles I selected are not meant to be "argumentative." Even the Amish do not always entirely agree with interpretations!

Surprisingly, the editors missed the fiftieth anniversary of the publication, as Joseph Stoll acknowledged in the Staff Notes in the June 2018 issue:

How can we explain that the fiftieth anniversary of *Family Life* was overlooked, and no mention has been made in the magazine? The only excuse I can think of is that we were too busy preparing this year's magazines, and forgot all about having completed fifty years.

The reminder came in the mail. A nice hand-drawn greeting from a family in Virginia . . . "Happy Birthday, *Family Life*! January 1968 to January of 2018, fifty years encouraging the daily faith of many . . ." None of us in 1968 imagined the fledgling paper would, fifty years later, have such a wide circulation. God has blessed our feeble efforts beyond our expectations.

In April 2004, Joseph Stoll wrote in the Staff Notes about the challenges of being an editor and concluded with these words, so indicative of the publication, which helped keep me going as I read through another twenty-five years of magazines:

We do the same things over and over. Just as a farmer keeps on milking his cows several times a day, seven days a week, so our labor continues as long as God grants us life and strength. We must press forward and keep on and not let the bumps hinder us from doing our duty.

Whether we are farmers, teachers, ministers (or even editors), there will be setbacks and moments of discouragement. We will make mistakes. Yet with God's help, let us keep on doing what needs to be done. How else can we keep the cows milked?

TWO

Amish Beginnings

THE AMISH AND MENNONITES are Anabaptists, or "re-baptizers," so called because they believe in adult rather than infant baptism. After Martin Luther triggered the Reformation, various Protestant churches formed in Europe, and 1525 saw the emergence of the Swiss Brethren in Zurich, Switzerland. Some had already been baptized in the state church as infants, and so baptized themselves again as adults in the new faith, hence the name. The Anabaptists considered themselves neither Catholic nor Protestant, which set the stage for conflict.

Considered radicals, thousands were tortured and put to death for their beliefs. Their nonviolent resistance to the authorities, and resulting imprisonment and punishment, is documented in books like the *Martyrs Mirror* (in print since 1660) and the *Ausbund* hymnbook (in print since 1564). Both remain a part of Amish faith and worship today.

The so-called New World was seen as a place where they might be allowed to worship freely, and many Anabaptists started arriving in Philadelphia in the early 1700s, after a long, perilous voyage across the Atlantic. Today, many Amish reflect on the persecution of their forebears and place a high value on keeping their Anabaptist heritage alive and relevant.

The Amish were not, and are not, frozen in time, but have had to adapt or adjust to the changing world and governments around them. Separation of church and state remains a thorny issue for the Amish, and over the years they have successfully dealt with issues around Social Security and mandatory education laws. But despite these modern challenges, the Amish population has continued to grow and spread at a dramatic rate.

The Anabaptist Vision, Revisited

In 1943, Goshen College historian Harold S. Bender gave a thirty-minute speech in New York City to the American Society of Church History. Before that, historians had regarded Anabaptists as a rather fanatical and radical element in the overall Reformation picture. This had never really bothered our Old Order people, since we had long been aware that some of our beliefs were looked down upon by the general public. Our forefathers were far more interested in being faithful than popular. As I understand it, Bender gave these focal points:

1. *Discipline as being basic to Christianity.*

Protestants placed an emphasis on Jesus' dying for our sins, so that we are now free from sin's penalty. We have no more guilt, and thus we enjoy peace with God. [The Anabaptist] focus was more on being a disciple of Christ. A disciple follows and obeys his Master. The primary word was not *faith*, as it was with [Martin] Luther, [John] Calvin, and [Ulrich] Zwingli, but *discipleship*. Faith cannot be separated from a godly life.

2. *The church as a covenanted, visible, holy brotherhood.*

The second point of significance was the role of the church in each believer's life. Infant baptism was a major issue in those days. But it was not the real cause of their disagreement. At baptism, Christian believers committed their lives to God, but also to the brotherhood as the guiding authority in matters of conduct. To be a voluntary member of the visible church presented a threat to the whole political and religious control of a territory. They refused to swear oaths, they would not take up arms, they would not have their infants baptized. In brief, they were nonconformists in the society of their day. That is why the local rulers reacted so strongly. Infant baptism brought everyone automatically into the governing system. But now, if an adult chose to be baptized and become a member of a church that was not a part of the state church, the whole system unraveled.

3. Love and nonresistance in all Christian relationships.
The third major difference was the Anabaptist stand on nonviolence and nonuse of force. Along with this was the Anabaptist vision of the church as a true brotherhood that practiced love to each other. Every Christian was obligated before God to supply the necessities of life to any of the brethren in need.

Anabaptism completely rejected the view that a Christian can take up arms and fight for the state. Under no circumstances can a follower of Christ do anything that is contrary to the spirit and example of his Master. He must separate himself from the world and its kingdom, and help create a Christian social order within the brotherhood.

—Rob R. Schlabach, August/September 2015

Between Two Extremes
The year 1993 was supposed to be a very special year for the Amish. You see, it marked the three hundredth anniversary of the Amish division of 1693. While Mennonite scholars and church officials were jetting off to Europe and to distant

states to attend conferences, give speeches, and autograph books about the division, we Amish gave very little notice to the event. I guess we have been too busy currying our horses, planting our gardens, and harvesting our grain to pay much attention to what happened three centuries ago.

We can think of the beginning of the Anabaptist movement in 1525, when our forefathers broke away from the state churches. The change was brought about not by those who were content to wait and see what happened, but by those who were courageous enough to stand up and be counted.

The example of the early Anabaptist martyrs' zeal is often held up to us. They were indeed men who were unafraid to proclaim the truth with boldness. But there is one thing that we can't discover from the church records they left: What kind of church members would they have made had they been allowed to live long enough? We do know that they were very opinionated, and not always of the same opinion. Within a few short years the Anabaptist movement had degenerated into many factions which were opposed to each other and widely separated on views of nonresistance, prophecy, salvation, and everyday life.

The zeal of [Conrad] Grebel, [Felix] Manz, [Jacob] Hutter, and [Balthasar] Hubmaier got things going, but the solidity of Menno Simons, Dietrich Philips, and Peter Riedemann allowed the movement to develop into a stable church. The Anabaptist movement died down nearly everywhere, except where these leaders worked.

Unfortunately, the passing of time again brought a certain degree of self-satisfied unconcern. When the leaders such as Menno had passed from the scene, other less devoted men took their place. Discipline relaxed, spirituality declined, and the spirit of materialism took hold. It was in such a setting that Jacob Ammann made his appearance in Alsace and

Switzerland. His message likely stirred the members into a fresh round of controversy.

Although little is really known about Jacob Ammann, most scholars would agree that he was a man of vision and purpose and full of zeal. Unfortunately, he was also a man with a sharp tongue and a hot head. Several years after the Amish division, Ammann and his followers realized that they had acted out of a wrong spirit. To make things right, they placed themselves under the ban and asked to be reconciled to their former church. However, since they were not willing to change their convictions on the issues, the attempted reconciliation failed, and the rift became final.

What is our reaction when we see drift in the church, or if things are let go without being dealt with? Do we shrink from speaking up because someone might be offended by it? Do we want to be discreet and not say too much because "the time is not right," or "it isn't bad enough yet," or "it isn't my responsibility"? Do we sometimes try to relabel cowardice as "modesty"?

If we ourselves are spiritually cold and possessed with a smug self-righteousness, we cannot possibly pass on the true biblical faith to our children, because we haven't got it ourselves. But if we are found with a critical spirit, and cannot exercise proper control over our tongues and emotions, we may fail just as badly.

—*A Searcher for the Happy Medium*, January 1994

* * *

A huge volume of more than a thousand pages, the *Martyrs Mirror* is rarely given the serious study it deserves. For one thing, it is so big that many readers are frightened away by the sheer size of it. From my own early childhood, I recall going away to visit with my parents, and observing a very practical use being made of this big book. At mealtime, it was often discovered that a little preschooler like myself couldn't reach the plate unless the *Martyrs Mirror* was placed on the bench for me to sit on!

In the past, the accounts in this book have inspired men and women to be steadfast in the faith, even unto death. The *Martyrs Mirror* has that potential still. Who knows what the future may hold? Even if our time of freedom continues, we need the message of the *Martyrs Mirror*.

—J. S., March 1997

Meet the Martyrs Mirror

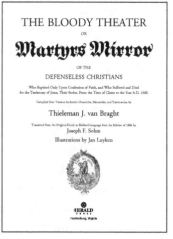

The Bloody Theater or Martyrs Mirror of the Defenseless Christians could be considered the most significant book to come out of the Anabaptist movement. However, the 1,157-page book remains unread by many people because of its great size. Interested persons know that it is valuable as both a historical and inspirational source, but it seems too big a book to try to read.

Why "bloody theater"?

Notice the words at the top of the title page: "The Bloody Theater." These can be related to several ideas in Scripture. The English word *theater* occurs in Scripture only in telling of the persecution of the early Christians. Paul says in 1 Corinthians 4:9, "For we are made a spectacle unto the world, and to angels, and to men." (For *spectacle*, the original Greek text was *theatron* from which we get our English word *theater*.)

Thus, we may connect the "theater" of the title page with the words from Scripture, and remember how the world has viewed Christians in anger and rejection. In fact, Christians became a source of entertainment, as they were put to death in Roman amphitheaters before bloodthirsty crowds of spectators.

What is a "martyr"?

The English word *martyr* is derived from the Greek word *martus* and its various forms depending on its usage. Originally it meant "witness." Near the end of the New Testament period of history, under the pressure of persecution, the word *martus* began to take on a new meaning. The word began to refer to those who witnessed for Christ not only with their words but also with their deaths. As persecution continued and more Christians gave their lives for the faith, this new meaning became more frequent, as is evident in the writings of the Apostolic Fathers.

Why a "mirror"?

When Thieleman J. van Braght compiled the *Martyrs Mirror*, the word *mirror* had several meanings. Besides the common meaning of "a surface that reflects light or images," it was often used to name a collection of writings on a particular subject.

But there is more to it than that. Terence, an ancient Roman writer, said, "I bid him look into the lives of men as though as into a mirror and from others to take an example for himself." This idea has continued to be associated with *mirror* down through time. As one definition for *mirror*, the *Oxford English Dictionary* gives "that which exhibits something to be imitated; an example . . . hence of persons, a model of excellence."

When van Braght decided to use the word *mirror* in his title, he probably had both meanings in mind: "a collection of writings on a subject" and "examples of persons to be imitated."

What are "defenseless Christians"?

Reading farther down the title page, we notice next the Christians who were "defenseless," a term sometimes used in the past century where we use *nonresistant* today. The mention of the defenseless Christians on the title page emphasizes the importance of the doctrine of nonresistance in this book. Defenselessness in the face of the attacks of evil in this present world has often resulted in suffering as the *Martyrs Mirror* testifies.

In conclusion

To summarize, the *Martyrs Mirror* has two parts. Part 1 has a single author, van Braght; part 2 has many authors, from the earliest Anabaptists in 1525—Felix Mantz, Michael Sattler, George Blaurock, and many others—down through the publication date of the book, 1660. Part 2 includes letters written by the martyrs, accounts of hearings, interrogations, court trials, eyewitness descriptions of executions of martyrs, and other material.

On pages 8–13, van Braght reveals that he believes that since persecution has ceased in the Netherlands, his church has declined from obedience to the truth. He hopes that by reading the accounts of the martyrs, the church can be challenged to renew its faith and zeal.

This is the challenge that van Braght offered his readers in 1660. This challenge has continued to be important to those who have reprinted this large volume so many times in English and German editions. For this reason, the book has been a recurring and enduring part of Amish/Mennonite/Hutterite history.

—James Lowry, March 1997

* * *

North American Printings of the Ausbund

On any given Sunday morning between nine and ten o'clock in thirty US states and one Canadian province, the "Loblied" is always being sung in hundreds of Amish church services. Its first line begins slowly. The tune rises and falls as the congregation sings the hymn of four seven-line stanzas, which takes twenty minutes or more.

The origin of the *Ausbund* dates back nearly five hundred years. In 1535, some Anabaptist refugees from Bavaria (today part of Germany) fled because of persecution to Moravia (today a region in the Czech Republic). During the summer, a decision was made that some of them would attempt to return to their homes in Bavaria. So a group of sixty Anabaptists left Moravia in August and traveled down the Danube River. They had barely set foot inside Bavarian territory when they were captured by the Catholic authorities from the city of Passau. They were taken to the bishop's castle and imprisoned in its dreary dungeons. That is where the *Ausbund* was born.

Since some of the prisoners apparently were good at compiling poetry, they wrote songs to comfort themselves and their brethren in bonds. Somehow the songs were written down, not merely memorized, for there were fifty-one, some exceptionally lengthy.

None of the prisoners were condemned to death; however, many were tortured and died because of this plus the miserable living conditions in the dungeons. In 1540, five years after their capture, the prisoners who were yet alive were released. No one knows who had the songs in his or her possession. All that is known is the songs safely left the Passau dungeon and were printed as a hymnal twenty-four years later in 1564, entitled *Etliche schöne Christliche Geseng*, not *Ausbund*.

This slender hymnal, which would become the backbone of today's thick *Ausbund*, was never reprinted. In fact, it was unknown until 1928, when Harold S. Bender, a Mennonite historian, discovered it in a bookstore in Harrisburg, Pennsylvania.

In 1693–94, the Swiss Anabaptists divided into two groups—the Amish with Jacob Ammann as their leader, and the Mennonites with Hans Reist as theirs. Both groups continued to sing from the updated editions of the *Auss Bundt*, and both brought their copies to America, where they settled in what today is Pennsylvania. The Reist Mennonites were the first to cross the Atlantic Ocean, arriving in 1710. They were followed by the Amish in the 1730s and later.

The *Ausbund* is the oldest hymnal in continuous use in congregational singing in the world. Although it has long been extinct in its European homeland, it is "alive and well" among the Amish. As of 2014, there have been fifty-nine printings in America [since 1935 in Lancaster, Pennsylvania]. A total of 157,919 were printed between 2000 and 2014 for an average 10,528 per printing.

—David Luthy, March 2015

Appreciating Our German Heritage
This article is a summary of a topic given at an Ontario summer school for teachers. The author was encouraged to submit this to *Family Life*.

Almost five hundred years have passed since the beginnings of the Anabaptists. All these years that faith has been passed on. Have you thought of something else that was passed down? It was German, of course. That language was passed from one generation to another. Almost all of us speak it. Most of our worship services are in German. It is our mother tongue.

So we have kept the faith and we have kept the language. Are those two isolated facts, or are they somehow connected? Did we try so hard to keep the faith that we automatically kept the language expressing it? Or did we keep the language and thereby kept the faith? I don't know. But I choose to believe that the two are interrelated. Language is the vehicle in which we express our faith.

Because language and faith are connected, I believe that if we lose the German, we lose a part of our heritage, and maybe some nuggets of our faith. Faith can be expressed in any language. When we received the faith, it was packaged in German. If we throw that packaging away, will we know when to stop throwing away?

It is possible to express conservative values, and scriptural principles and doctrines, in English just as well as in German. German is not holy. English is not corrupt. But by sticking to the old German language and songs, we go back before the Protestant influences became so prevalent.

The Epistles speak frequently of a separation from the world. One part of our separation is our mother tongue. Separation in language is not the aim; it just helps us to be separate. The downside of this is that our separate language becomes a barrier to outsiders when they want to worship with us.

Another reason to retain our German is that it keeps us traditional. A tradition by itself is not good nor bad. It is like a train track. The track keeps the train going in the right direction. A tradition of language keeps us connected to former values. Speaking German does not make us moral. But as society's morals decay and corrupt, German is one of the building blocks that help keep us separate from that decay and corruption.

If our reasons to keep the German are too shallow, we may lose this part of our heritage. There is no greater hypocrite than one who extols his heritage but doesn't live by it. Part of our heritage is German. Let us appreciate it enough to live by it.

—Amsey Martin, January 2015

Is the Back Door Open?

I will try to give a brief outline of the conditions that led to our wanting to be separate from the public schools.

Sometime after 1920, the age of mandatory attendance in the state of Ohio was raised to sixteen. But for another twenty-five years or so, this was not enforced, especially not in rural country schools.

However, as industrialization spread out into rural America, there was a greater awareness by local school officials of the need for more education so that young people would be better trained in specialized and technical skills. Also, as the percentage of nonfarm families increased, more and more children had leisure time on their hands when not in school.

Then as the automotive age came in, school buses made it possible for schools to be consolidated, even in rural areas. After the Depression and World War II were over, the economy grew much stronger. The alienation from the land and the exodus to the cities continued at an even faster pace.

Already in the 1920s (Delaware) and 1930s (Pennsylvania), there had been a few isolated incidents where Amish resisted the obvious trends of the day, with the result that several parochial schools were established.

It was when local officials tried to enforce attendance to the age of sixteen, which among other things meant going to high school, that problems became much more urgent and pronounced. Almost at this same time (late 1940s and early 1950s), the officials sought to close down the one-room country schools and bus the children to town schools. This was called consolidation.

In these new and expanded schools, there were large gymnasiums to accommodate a physical education program and, naturally, a much fuller sports schedule. Most non-Amish children by this time had no chores, did not walk to school, and attended classes until they were nearly adults, and the textbooks and teachers refrained from any Bible instruction. Moreover, the radio and car had led to increased interest in professional sports.

It was rightly perceived by Amish parents and church leaders that these changes in public schools were a threat to their beliefs and practices. At times, there was enough solid, determined resistance to these issues to result in Amish parents being jailed.

Looking back now on these events, it is clear that the firm stand that was taken and the willingness to suffer going to jail is what really set things in motion, and led some twenty years later to the Supreme Court ruling [*Wisconsin v. Yoder*, 1972] that gave us the full legal privilege to have our own schools.

A half century or more has passed since the Amish school movement began in earnest. What were the issues that caused conflict back then? Let us review at least four of the main ones:

1. High school attendance
2. Large, consolidated schools
3. The teaching of science
4. Organized sports

We do well to pause and take inventory of how we today measure up with regard to these issues. Are we standing firm on the principles for which our parents and grandparents struggled?

Today we once again have textbooks that teach morals as well as academic skills. We have been able to develop a curriculum that is better suited to our needs. We continue with elementary schools that provide our children with an eighth-grade education. Our teachers as a whole have proven themselves quite competent in conducting classes to that level.

As for finances, our schools operate at approximately 10 percent of the budget public schools have. That includes erecting new buildings as required.

Nearly all our pupils walk to one-room or two-room schools. The use of school buses often nearly doubles the cost of education, and who knows, often about doubles the problems as well. We can be thankful we can do without.

However, there are also changes taking place in our community that cause concern and alarm. In many families, it has become harder for an eighth-grade graduate to learn good work habits since there is often no work at home. As our shop owners let their businesses grow large, and with the increased use of technology, they can get into quite sophisticated production and marketing strategies and use more scientific methods common to industry. This could well be the backdoor opening to higher education that was refused at the front door by our grandparents two generations ago.

—Rob R. Schlabach, October 2005

* * *

Amish Settlements across America
People sometimes assume that the Amish population might be dying out, but there could be nothing further from the truth.

If you really like to meet people and you really like to travel, have you ever imagined what it would be like to visit a different Amish church district every Sunday, and how long it would take you to visit them all? It would take you at least twenty-one years to make the rounds of existing church districts.

But wait a minute. Don't think that you would be finished then. No, not at all. The present rate of growth is one new settlement every month and a new Amish church district about every nine days! The Amish population has been doubling every twenty years. This means that by the end of the twenty-one years, you would be further behind than when you started. If the world stands and our churches continue to grow at the present rate, you would never catch up!

In my lifetime the number of church districts has doubled itself more than three times, from 131 districts in 1935 to 1,076 today. There were then 41 settlements in fifteen states and one province [of Canada], compared to 267 settlements today in twenty-four states and one province. In other words, there are now *eight* times as many Amish as when I was born.

—Joseph Stoll, May 1997

One cannot help but wonder what the numbers and geographic distribution would be if a major church division had not occurred during the last half of the 1800s. At least 50 percent of the Amish at that time are thought not to have remained with the "old order" and eventually were absorbed into the Mennonite church.

By 1851, when obvious cracks were appearing in Amish church unity, Bishop David Beiler of Lancaster County, Pennsylvania, suggested having a nationwide ministers' meeting (*Diener-Versammlung*) at which the ministry "could make oral inquiry and give a directive." Eleven years would pass before such a meeting occurred; and when it did, Beiler and many other traditional-minded ministers did not attend.

In 1862, the first of sixteen annual meetings (1862–76, 1878) was held. In reality, the meetings did not restore unity, but resulted in a division into two main groups: (1) the Old

Order Amish who wished to retain the traditions of their fore-fathers, and (2) the change-minded Amish Mennonites, also nicknamed "meetinghouse Amish," because they erected meetinghouses instead of continuing to gather for worship services in houses and barns.

—David Luthy, June 2000

Never before have Amish resided in so many states. New settlements have been founded in Colorado, Idaho, Maine, Nebraska, and Washington, in which states no Amish were residing when the former 1997 directory was published. Thus, by midsummer 2003 there were settlements in twenty-eight US states and one Canadian province.

That the Amish are migrating into new areas is best illustrated by the fact that of the 333 settlements existing in July 2003, nearly half of them, or 157, were founded since 1990.

Because of the rising price of land, most potential buyers cannot afford to buy an entire farm and are glad many farms are being divided into parcels and auctioned off that way. It also means they can stay in the home community and not have to join the exodus to new settlements where land is cheaper than in the older, well-established communities.

The splitting of farms into parcels does not always mean the buyers will not be farmers. More and more farmers are making a living on less acreage by raising produce and fruits. However, it is a fact that the general trend in many settlements is away from farming to home businesses, such as engine shops, metal fabricating, welding, stove manufacturing, and especially woodworking. These latter shops make a great variety of items, from furniture to storage sheds to mailboxes. In some communities most men work at Amish-owned saw-mills. In others they work in trailer factories or as day laborers in various occupations.

The number of congregations or church districts at midsummer 2003 totaled 1,408—an increase of 311 since December 1996. Ohio leads with 375 districts, followed by Pennsylvania with 312, and Indiana with 246. These three states have 66 percent of the districts, which means they have two-thirds of the Amish population.

—David Luthy, October 2003

An updated directory as of October 31, 2013, has been compiled, reflecting more dramatic growth. The number of settlements in five years' time has grown from 388 to 473—an increase of 85, or a new settlement about every three weeks. Pennsylvania has the most settlements with 55, followed closely by Ohio with 54. New York has 50, followed by Wisconsin with 49. Michigan has 39; Missouri, 38; Kentucky, 36; Indiana, 23; and Iowa, 22. Twenty other states and one Canadian province account for the other 107 settlements.

The number of congregations or church districts has risen from 1,679 to 2,012—an increase of 333. Ohio continues to have the most with 475, followed by Pennsylvania with 430, and Indiana with 336.

These statistics were compiled with the assistance of Joseph Donnermeyer, a professor at Ohio State University.

—David Luthy and Joseph Donnermeyer, January 2014

From Sea to Sea

Our family took a special interest in the recent survey of Amish settlements across the United States and in Ontario. Now let us envision our Sunday services. Starting in Delaware or Maine, we begin singing the "Loblied" [in the *Aushund*]. Its notes rise in unison and gradually move westward across Pennsylvania, Ohio, Indiana. Finally the last notes end in Idaho. On through each time zone, there is singing of the

"Loblied," hour after hour, and our Father in heaven listens to this. Are we putting our hearts into the words? It is all so sacred and inspiring!

—*A grateful grandmother*, March 2014

THREE

Living in the Present

IT IS EASY TO LOOK AT THE AMISH, with their uniform dress and horse and buggies, and assume nothing has changed very much in their way of life. But it has. One mistake we "English" (non-Amish) make is to see this as a lifestyle. But it is a religion from which everything else flows. It may appear to be just a bunch of strict rules to follow, but there is a surprising diversity to the ways Amish live across the United States and Canada. And there is sometimes disagreement on how to adjust to the modern world. What does it mean to be Plain? What is a "simple" way of life?

The modern world continuously makes its influence known. How to respond is a challenge. What about the young people? Is life too easy? Does the grass seem greener elsewhere? These are all questions the Amish share with us, although the response is different. And when the COVID-19 pandemic came, we were all thrust into a very different world. Although the editors of *Family Life* acknowledged the pandemic, they chose to keep discussion out of the magazine, citing much misinformation. Perhaps we could learn a few things from their approach to the world around them, which takes them away from social media, television, livestreaming, and the internet.

Simple Living: How Can We Keep It?

How can we instill in our children the value of the Plain life? We treasure the simplicity of our heritage, and although we know it is not the key to eternal life, we feel plainness is a necessary fruit—evidence that we have set our affection on things eternal. How can we hope to stem the tide of worldliness?

As parents, we have a tremendous influence on our children. Surely there are some things we can do to guide them in the way we would have them go. Praying for our children must be the most important thing we can do—so important that it almost goes without saying. Next to that, we need to have our reasons for Plain living rooted in the right place, and not merely because of church standards. Our example is another key. We need to consistently practice simple living in our homes, our clothing, and our activities. No part of our life is lost to the keen perception of our children. They are quick to notice hypocrisy—and despise it.

Unless we are truly humble, we are not truly Plain. We should avoid exposing our children needlessly to modernism. We also have to specifically teach our children to live plainly. They need solid reasons for doing or avoiding things, not merely a careless "this is how we do it" answer. Eventually they should be able to see that the luxuries and complexities of the world are a hindrance to our faith.

There is a prevalent fear that in promoting plainness, we cultivate a better-than-thou attitude. Although there is a danger in this, we dare not use it as an excuse to drift with the tide. There is no need for us to criticize others for not measuring up to our standards. If our attitude toward those with worldlier standards of living is one of concern and disappointment, rather than criticism and scorn, our children can also learn to live plainly without looking down on those who don't.

Besides all these things, we should not leave our children with the false impression that we have no temptation in this line. But we must also help them see that the trend toward what is bigger, fancier, and more expensive leads rapidly in one direction—away from God.

—*An Observant Parent*, May 1997

A Million Dollars

In one of our reading books, there is a story called "The Hundred-Thousand-Dollar Boy." Two young lads were complaining about their lot in life. Because they were from poor families, they could not have all the things that other boys had. Finally, the father of one of the boys came upon the scene and began to ask his son some questions.

"Would you take $10,000 for your legs?" he asked.

His son said no, for he needed his legs to run and jump.

"Would you take $10,000 for your arms?"

Again the son refused. The father then proceeded to ask about his eyes, his voice, his hearing, his sense of taste, and his health. Each time the son was not willing to part with it, even for a large sum of money.

Finally, at the end of the story, Dad figured up that his son was worth at least $100,000! And the son realized how very rich he actually was. We are so used to measuring everything by money that perhaps this is the only way to get our message across.

My mind goes to people who have become dissatisfied with our Amish lifestyle and our way of applying Christian principles to everyday living. They usually degrade our strict standards and justify their change to a more liberal society where there is more freedom of personal expression.

I have to wonder, are these values of ours not worth clinging to? Are they not worth preserving? I think they are. Should we attempt to place a monetary value on certain principles so we appreciate them more? Why don't we try it?

1. Amish do not divorce. Children grow up within the security of a family, knowing where they belong. What is this influence and stability worth to a child? Let's set a price on this at $100,000. (Luke 16:18; 1 Corinthians 7:10)

2. The mothers are keepers of the home. They are with the families and take care of the children. The influence of a godly mother, who can measure it? Better set this at $200,000. (2 Timothy 1:5; Titus 2:4–5)

3. Our children are taught to stick to a job until it is done. It seems that one of the biggest problems in the world is finding people who are willing to work hard for a decent wage. This learning to work with our hands and the sweat of the face, what is it worth? Let's value this one at $100,000. (1 Thessalonians 4:11; 2 Thessalonians 3:10)

4. I once read in a newspaper that a big problem among today's youth is that they are bored. This is astonishing. They probably have elaborate homes, the best cars, color TV, and everything else that goes with the modern life. Yet they are bored.

I would think Amish children have a big advantage. For one thing, they are used to being part of a large family. Thus, they learn much about companionship, sharing unselfishly, and getting along with others. Plus, look at all the things there are to do. Girls learn about cooking and sewing, working in the garden, and hundreds of other things. Boys learn about shopwork, the farm chores, how to drive a team of horses, and other skills. Besides, there are the woods and streams to explore, and the birds and flowers and wild animals to enjoy. Growing up in this kind of environment, what is it worth? $50,000? (1 John 2:15; Psalm 104:24)

5. We are a bilingual people, which means we speak two languages. (Or is it trilingual—Pennsylvania German, English, and High German?) We are used to it and perhaps take this privilege too much for granted.

Strange as it may seem, most of the people who leave our Amish society for a more liberal one attach little value to knowing a second language, and they themselves or their descendants soon lose it. $50,000. (Acts 21:40)

6. Recently, I took special notice of three young girls in church who were preparing for baptism. They were dressed modestly in uniform attire. Our churches, separated from the world and made up of members who care for each other—this is worth a great deal. $200,000. (Hebrews 13:17; 1 Peter 3:3–5)

7. The young people are taught purity. They can come together in a marriage as man and wife in a proper biblical way. They do not need to have memories of relationships with other partners [that may] mar the beauty of their marriage. Let's set the value of this at $100,000. (1 Thessalonians 4:3–5; 2 Corinthians 6:15–20)

8. The Amish are accustomed to visiting others and to welcoming visitors into their homes at any time. It is an extra treat when someone from out of state comes by and stays for the night. This practice has been largely lost in modern-day homes, and people have become dependent on motels and restaurants. It is said that city people who live as next-door neighbors often do not know each other. The virtue of entertaining strangers and of visiting back and forth, let's value it at $50,000. (1 Peter 4:9; Hebrews 13:2)

9. Our people are sensitive to each other's needs. It is touching to see how quickly neighbors gather to help when there has been a death or when a barn burns down. Surely this is something we don't want to lose. $100,000. (Galatians 6:2; James 1:27)

10. The Amish care for their own older people instead of pushing them into nursing homes. Being kind to our grandparents in their sunset years can be a real blessing, both to them and to the rest of us. Knowing that our own children will take care of us, too, when we get old and helpless—this is a comforting thought. $50,000. (Leviticus 19:32; 1 Thessalonians 5:14; 1 Timothy 5:8)

We have tried to list a few outstanding virtues and values. There might well be other groups who hold to these values as faithfully as we do. Perhaps more faithfully. We wish them God's blessings.

There may also be Amish communities where some of these values have been lost. This is sad. The important question for you and me is this—Are we diligently striving, with God's help, to uphold these virtues? Or are we lax and unconcerned? (2 Peter 1:5)

—John Lambright, June 1993

Must We?

> Must we spend so much on houses,
> Stately mansions built just so,
> When the homeless of the world
> Haven't any place to go?
>
> Must we have such lovely kitchens,
> Costly cabinets wall to wall,
> When the starving of the world
> Haven't any food at all?
>
> Must our homes be furnished grandly,
> Fancy trinkets here and there,
> When the shivering of the world
> Haven't any clothes to wear?

When we come to that great Judgment,
　　What will Jesus' verdict be?
"Lo, as unto these my brethren,
　　Ye have done it unto me."

Though we may be ardent givers
　　To the needy of our day,
Must we still, in lavish spending,
　　Live so richly anyway?

Does it look like here's our heaven
　　In this earthly life so dear?
Let us learn to live more simply,
　　For our homeland is not here.

　　　　　　　　　　　　　　—M. J. M., June 2003

The Picture

I have a copy of the Pulitzer Prize–winning photograph Kevin Carter took of a vulture stalking a starving child. These two create a silent scene that is chilling in the extreme, because no one can doubt what the outcome will be.

When I think about that little child in the picture, I always am left with more questions than answers. And when I think too deeply, I become uncomfortable. Uncomfortable, maybe, because I remember the African man who commented to an American, "In my country people die because they have no food to eat. In your country they die because they eat too much food."

It makes me ashamed that I have so much. How can I justify my affluence when so many people die for want of food, clean water, medicines, shelter, all the things that I take for granted?

But wait a minute. Affluent. Is that the word I want? We're not rich. In fact, it's generally a challenge to yank the ends together financially to pay all the bills. We live on an amount of money that those who file our taxes call low-income.

And then I realized that whether I admit it or not, we are prosperous indeed. Our house is large and warm and clean and full of so many things. What we consider the basic necessities—food, bathrooms, bedrooms, clean water at the sink, and even having a sink—are still luxuries to many more people than not. Where is justice in a world where children die from lack of food, and I weigh more than I should from consuming more calories than I need?

How can I love God and not give more to those who are hungry, those who have so little? Even in America, while I feed my children, thousands more cry because they lack food, or shelter, or both. I could spend less on wants, luxuries even, and give more. Mostly I just don't want to deny myself in order to give more.

And my second excuse. I use it sometimes, too, by telling myself I can give so little. A handful of twenties a year. A ten or two here and there. That's completely insignificant in the vast sea of human need, so little I might as well keep it and spend it for something we want.

I know I must begin to change my thinking if I want to change my ways. No, I can't remove world hunger. I can't end war or disease or suffering. But it's time I stopped excusing myself because I can do so little, and do the little I can.

—Anonymous, May 2015

Life Is Just Not Fair

Why is it that I live in a land of plenty and have so much food—even some to throw away—and others go to bed hungry?

Why is it that I have more clothes than I really need when others long for something to protect them from the biting cold?

Why is it that I have a Christian home when so many children live deserted on the streets, crying for want of love?

Why is it that I am blessed with clear eyesight while others grope in a world of darkness?

Why is it that I can walk almost without effort while some people patiently endure the confines of a wheelchair?

Why is it that I enjoy the gift of hearing while others have no idea what the sweet strains of singing sound like?

Why is it that I may be part of a caring Christian brotherhood when others have never even heard of God's love?

Why is it that I am allowed to freely worship God while others are imprisoned for their faith?

God has richly blessed me. Am I truly thankful?

—Anonymous, June 2008

* * *

The Sickness Book

A list of common elements of the spirit and soul, with recommended cures and treatments:

1. *Green Grass Fever:* This strange ailment is also known as "Discontentment Syndrome," and in some communities as "Moving Fever."

Symptoms: The symptoms are varied, but there is nearly always some distortion of vision. The side effects are unhappiness, discontent, and a lack of appreciation for an existing situation. The disease may be very contagious, spreading through a community like a prairie fire. Fortunately, some people are immune to the germ.

Prognosis: The disease often runs its course, without a relapse. Other times, though, it will keep recurring so that as soon as one bout is past, another is liable to begin.

Treatment: There is no miracle cure, but treatment is usually effective if the patient is willing to submit to therapy. Often the simplest cure is to hold still, and the disease may run its course in a matter of weeks. Nonetheless, the patient should be treated—generally in a session with older or wiser people who by their advice will be able to lower the fever and arrest the disease.

2. *Hardening of the Conscience:* Unlike hardening of the arteries, this disease is as likely to attack the young as the old. It is a progressive disease and never occurs suddenly; it must have time to develop. The cause is well known and is self-inflicted—abuse of the conscience. Ignoring and disregarding the conscience causes it to become calloused and hardened.

Symptoms: The sense of right and wrong becomes clouded, and the ability to act upon the right is weakened.

Prognosis: If the disease is treated in its early stages, the outlook is fairly bright. The patient must cooperate, however, and repent of his past misuse of his conscience. If the disease is far advanced, the chances of recovery are slight. In extreme cases there is no known cure.

3. *Money Grippe:* A very common disease, and church members are not immune to it. The disease is a cancer that grows slowly and stealthily, and some people are seriously ill before they become aware of their condition. If left untreated, this disease eventually claims a choking grip on a man's life and soul, smothering his desire to serve God.

Symptoms: Money and riches become important. There are signs of greed and avarice. The victim exhibits a selfish spirit, taking advantage of others in business deals. He may become a workaholic. He derives extreme pleasure and satisfaction from the increase of his riches.

Prognosis: The outlook is not good at all. If the disease is not arrested, it is invariably fatal to the soul.

4. *Spinal Deficiency:* Also known as "Weak Backbone" or "Jellyfish Disease." This condition is observed in all age groups,

but is especially common among adolescents where peer pressure and immaturity have a weakening effect on the spine. The disease becomes dangerous under the influence of evil companions. Spinal Deficiency victims are unable to withstand temptation. They fall for any new thing. They have no moral integrity of their own and are dependent on the standards set by others.

Treatment: Control of this disease lies not so much in treatment as in prevention. Boys and girls must be nurtured to build a strong character, and are immunized against this disease by having obedience and responsibility instilled at a tender age. They must learn to submit to authority—to their parents, teachers, ministers, and ultimately God.

5. *Talebearer's Itch:* Other names for this rather common affliction are "Gossip Disease" or "Wagging Tongue Syndrome." It is especially prevalent where crowds gather and where minds are not profitably occupied. Some people consider it as primarily a woman's disease, but this is not true. Many men also contract the germ.

People with low self-esteem are particularly vulnerable. Patients may be obsessed with the mistaken belief that lowering someone else's reputation will somehow elevate their own. In reality, just the opposite is true. Talebearer's Itch has destroyed many a reputation, but none so surely as the gossiper's own.

Symptoms: There is a perverted appetite for juicy tidbits of gossip, and a compulsive urge to share these with others. The result is the sowing of discord among brethren, and the separating of friends from each other.

Some textbooks claim that the disease can be confirmed by examining the tongue to see if it is abnormally sharp. Yet these outward signs can be misleading. The infection is always internal, and should be treated as such. The change of the heart's attitude is the only successful remedy.

Thus we conclude this brief catalog of spiritual ills that are common to mankind. In every instance, it is advisable to turn to the Great Physician for healing.

—Anonymous, April 2006

* * *

What Is Forgiveness?

We cannot change the events or the people who have wounded us, but God can help us avoid becoming bitter toward them. Failing to forgive locks us emotionally, and we are no longer able to properly respond to that individual. Forgiveness frees us from the bitterness and resentment that Satan would use to destroy us.

Our first instinct after being hurt is to build resentment. But we often fail to see that emotional response for what it really is—a spiritual problem. It is so much easier to focus on others' faults, identifying their shortcomings instead of our own.

Cleansing the resentment from our hearts is an opening process. Recognizing the problem is 90 percent of the solution. We need to take responsibility for our bitterness. Blamers are losers.

Nobody can make you angry—it is your choice. Anger resists healing; sorrow invites healing.

When pain is inflicted deeply into the heart, it cannot be forgiven and forgotten in a moment. Time and again, certain remarks or the sight of certain things will stir memories and bring back that heart-wrenching pain. But then we need to forgive again, up to seventy times seven, if necessary. Forgiveness happens as often as reminders of the hurt return.

Forgiveness means refusing to harbor feelings of ill will and bitterness. Never allow yourself to dwell on the injustice. Instead, commit your pain to God, asking for love and

forgiveness toward your fellow men. Love is enduring and kind.
It judges with the heart, and not with the mind.

—Anonymous, December 2013

Last summer we had a problem with stealing at our self-serve
produce stand. After considering the welfare of this man's soul,
I did not feel free to ignore the stealing. I wrote a letter, plead-
ing with him to quit his downward path. I told him we'd gladly
help him if he was in need. He would only need to come to the
house with his requests. We would give him what he needed,
and his conscience would be free.

The letter was laid out beside the cash box, but no one
showed up at the house. Respect for the produce stand was one
hundred percent the rest of the summer.

—*Old Order Mennonite*, June 2017

* * *

A Wake-Up Call to the World

Is *pandemic* a new word in your vocabulary? I'm sure we are all
familiar with the word *epidemic*, but now we hear of something
even worse, a *pandemic*. This is an epidemic of worldwide scope.
Such is the present COVID-19 crisis, an outbreak of a new virus that began in China and is spreading throughout the world.

For most of our readers, this is a brand-new experience. In
fact, the younger generation may not realize that such things
have happened before. Although it was years before my time, I
am aware of a pandemic that spread throughout the world just
as World War I came to a close, a little more than a hundred
years ago.

They called it the Spanish influenza, although no one has
ever proved that it began in Spain. Seldom has a virus been so
deadly. World War I had cost the lives of millions of soldiers

and civilians. But the flu that followed in its aftermath claimed far more victims than the war. An article in the *World Book Encyclopedia* sets the estimate at twenty million deaths worldwide, and half a million in the United States alone. Many people died of secondary complications, such as pneumonia and bronchitis.

The terrible pandemic of 1918–19 has a personal interest for me. Even though I was not born until a generation later, the Spanish influenza had a lasting effect on my family. It took the life of my grandmother at the age of forty-two. It left my father at the age of six to grow up in a motherless home, as well as his eleven brothers and sisters.

How did the public react to the Spanish influenza of 1918–19? From Sugarcreek, Ohio, came the report "Churches and schools are all closed because of influenza." A letter in the *Budget* from Daviess County reported on October 20, 1918, "We didn't have church for the last two Sundays on account of the influenza being spread around towns. The schools are also closed." Newspapers carried warnings on how to avoid the deadly flu. Some of the advice sounds amazingly familiar.

COVID-19 is a wake-up call to the whole world, and has brought many people to do some deep thinking. The COVID-19 crisis has disrupted the lives of all of us to some degree. The situation is rendered more confusing by the vast number of theories that are circulating, some true, some obviously false. Because of so much unconfirmed propaganda and the fast-changing scene, we decided on a general policy to not give much coverage to the whole coronavirus topic.

—J. S., excerpts from May, June, and October 2020

FOUR

Marriage and Family

THE EDITORS NAMED THEIR MAGAZINE *Family Life* for a reason. Along with religion, family and community are an integral part of being Amish. When I lived and worked on an Amish farm for a few months, I experienced a closeness and sense of belonging that I did not always find on the outside. In this section, I wanted to look at these relationships as the Amish would like them to be. (We will look at some of the problems in later chapters.) We do need to know the goal if we are to adequately measure our success and our failures in living up to the "ideal." Large families, typical of the Amish, bring a unique set of challenges. Submission may be a difficult concept for some to accept. Since the Amish do not permit divorce, there is often more work to do in sustaining a happy marriage, especially when the ideal and the real collide. And readers may be surprised that the Amish do adopt children sometimes, which brings its own set of concerns.

Marriage

The Joining of Two Streams

At a wedding we attended some time ago, the minister compared the joining of two lives with two streams coming together and forming a larger one. He said no matter how gently the waters flow, their joining causes some ripples. But thankfully, a short distance down the stream, the ripples have often disappeared and the waters are calm and peaceful again. The two streams are now one, blended in such a way that it is impossible to distinguish one from the other.

The minister's comparison did not stop there. No creek bed is perfectly smooth. There are rocks, fallen logs, drop-offs, and other obstacles that cause ripples and foam, and even at times turmoil. In the same way, no marriage is without its little hurts and doubts and pressures and misunderstandings that need to be worked out to keep it running smoothly and peacefully.

—The editors, February 1993

A Sobering Responsibility

To be a Christian husband and father in today's world is an awesome assignment. The responsibility is nearly overwhelming. How can I be the husband that my wife deserves, and the father that my family needs? Surely this should drive us to our knees in prayer, asking God for direction and divine guidance lest we fail our duty and neglect our God-given responsibility.

Why is this such a serious challenge? It is because of the far-reaching effects my conduct, as the head of the home, will have on the family. Will the children, when they reach the age of accountability, choose the right, and become a building member of the church? Or will they have developed an attitude of looking out for themselves, and choose rather to live in sin?

In most cases, a man hardly realizes the depth of his responsibility as he steps into marriage and fatherhood. Gradually as the duties and obligations increase, the seriousness penetrates to his very core and he cannot help but be humbled by it. Blessed is the man who comes to this realization early in his married life—while the children are still young and impressionable. If there is a delay and the children are already older, it becomes much more difficult to mold their characters and to lead them in the way they should go.

The order of headship

As the Scriptures teach us so clearly, the man is to be the head of the wife and the wife is to be submissive to her husband. The concept of the man being the head of the wife is today often misunderstood, and just as often misapplied. In the modern world this order of headship is widely ignored and scoffed at. Women demand equal rights. Submission to one's husband is an idea that is old-fashioned and outdated—modern women cannot accept such a role.

The weaker vessel

The apostle Paul gives us husbands some specific instructions how we should treat our wives: "Likewise, ye husbands, dwell with them according to knowledge, giving honour unto the wife, as unto the weaker vessel, and as being heirs together of the grace of life; that your prayers be not hindered" (1 Peter 3:7).

This passage contains a real challenge for Christian husbands, does it not? No suggestion here of the stern overbearing type of husband who is determined to rule his house with an iron hand.

On the other hand, we cannot feel this passage contradicts the opening verse of the same chapter, "Ye wives, be in subjection to your own husbands." Instead, the two thoughts—the wife's subjection to her husband and the husband's honor to the wife—complement each other perfectly. Each is a part of the whole—a harmonious relationship in a Christian marriage.

Finding a solution

When we were first married I wouldn't have thought my wife and I would ever disagree on points of any importance. Yet experience has shown that this can indeed occur. And when it does happen, and each one is convinced of being right, the matter needs to be taken to the Lord in prayer. A peaceable solution must be sought.

I as a husband must be ready to admit and to accept it when my wife has better reasons than my own, or when she is right and I am wrong. Her ideas may be more suitable or practical than mine. We must accept this, not begrudgingly, but give ourselves up completely to the will of God.

If however the husband still feels his thinking and reasoning is supported by the Word, he must seek to explain it once more in a spirit of honor and love, not in a spirit of authority or having the last word.

Once agreement is thus reached, only then can the decision be presented to the children, or to whomever it concerns, and the Lord's blessings can rest on it. If we allow our selfish nature to control our lives, that is what our children will learn from us. I have heard the saying "The eye learns better than the ear." In other words, attitudes are more often caught than taught.

In summing this up, being a responsible husband and father is awesome. Not taking this responsibility is tragic.

—Anonymous, February 1996

The Ideal Family

Part 1: The husband

What is an ideal man?

First and foremost he is a dedicated Christian who is sincerely trying to follow in Christ's footsteps of love, kindness, patience, and humility.

Such a man loves and respects his wife as his chosen helpmeet. He cherishes her in every way. Her opinion matters in the decisions that he must make.

He spends time in daily devotions with the family, reading Scriptures, praying, or singing praises to God.

He communicates well with others, especially with his wife and children, even if this sometimes means being the listener instead of the speaker.

Not once would he be seen beating a helpless child or animal in anger.

He is polite and courteous to all. He thanks his wife for preparing a tasty meal, even if she made soup and he'd craved ham, mashed potatoes, and gravy all afternoon at work.

He provides fair and consistent discipline for his children. They would not doubt his love for them, for he would take time to play a game of pitch and catch, or read a book to them.

He has a keen sense of humor. Not the distasteful type of humor, but an optimistic view of the unexpected twists that life can take.

Realizing his role as provider, he cheerfully finances necessary medical and dental care for his wife and children.

Once in a while he proves himself man enough to get his big hands in soapy dishwater—and gentle enough to change a baby's diaper.

He tries to keep the wash machine and the lawn mower maintained, because although his wife is capable and hardworking, the mysteries of a malfunctioning Briggs and Stratton [engine] are beyond her abilities.

That auction on Saturday really tempts him, but upon thinking it over, he admits he has no business spending borrowed money. He decides to stay at home and mow the yard, since the children are sick and his wife is busy.

His form of occupation isn't all that important, only that he is hardworking and tidy and a good provider. He does his best to manage carefully the money entrusted to them, and is willing to assist the needy with funds, or to lend a helping hand in the community.

Part 2: The ideal wife

The wife of such a man is of course a Christian too. She is a new creature in Christ and diligently seeks his guidance and the virtues of love, meekness, temperance, patience, and humility.

She loves and respects the man she married as the head of the home, but she is mature enough not to depend on him for happiness. With Christ she knows true peace, so she doesn't think that every little earthly detail has to be perfect before she can be happy.

Her clothes are plain, neat, and modest. The new clothes she wears don't have to be the latest crepe fabric or the rave of the neighboring community.

She strives to keep a reasonably clean and tidy house. Her tired husband must not often come to the door and find chaos in the kitchen.

Occasionally she takes time to prepare a cold drink and a snack for her husband when he's working hard—even if he's cleaning out the pigpen and smells not unlike a pig himself.

When he's depressed because the bills are coming in twice as fast as the paychecks, she listens quietly and then assures him that better days are coming.

She cheerfully makes a few pies for the local volunteer fire department bake sale. After all, it's the least she can do in appreciation for the folks who sacrificed their time and risk their lives to fight fires.

The meals she serves are usually tasty and nutritious. She's talented at using what fits the food budget in such a way that her family won't realize that they've had green beans three times a week.

Although she enjoys a trip now and then, she's also content to stay at home and enjoy life's quiet beauties, such as a brilliant sunset, a picnic at the creek, or a peaceful walk alone.

Her husband loves dogs, and the children have inherited that. So she consents to the rambunctious puppy that the neighbors gave. Her tulip bed is uprooted three days in a row, but she grits her teeth and reminds herself that even puppies grow up fast and that the children never had such a good playmate before.

She does the housework first, but doesn't begrudge herself an hour of good reading now and then.

When she has to have a hired girl, she treats her kindly, and doesn't allow the children to be rude and bossy to her.

She tries to "live and let live," even when this means forgiving the nearest and dearest ones over and over for their shortcomings.

—*An observer*, October 2001

Building a Christian Marriage

In today's society, there is a very high divorce rate. Even among churchgoing people, divorce has come to be well accepted. But before we feel smug that this is not at all true among our Plain people, let us take a look at the many unhappy marriages in our circles. How much better than a divorce is a marriage filled with constant arguments and hard feelings?

Building a good marriage is a lot like laying blocks. A crew of three can lay blocks very efficiently if they work together in harmony. When it comes to building a marriage, let us think of the three as being the husband, the wife, and Jesus. For any crew to run smoothly, it needs a rank of authority. Jesus is the head and also the one who will reward us when our work is done. The husband is the foreman, and the wife is the assistant.

Now let's consider that every time we do a good deed for our marriage partner, we are laying a building block. Love is the mortar that holds things together. We humans, of course, are prone to mistakes. We are bound to miss some good opportunities to lay blocks. We can create a happy marriage, not by never missing any blocks, but by working together to build a strong wall so that our children can follow our example.

Missed opportunities appear much more obvious and glaring to our spouse than to ourselves. So if our spouse misses a lot of blocks, what are we going to do about it? Actually, we have four options—two of which are acceptable, and two which are not.

Option #1—Forgiveness: We can choose to forgive, and trust our spouse to do better next time. This is a good option for minor incidents, such as when the husband is late for dinner or the wife spends more money at the dry goods store than she should have.

Option #2—Communication: If the problem is more serious, we can pick up the missed block and show it to our spouse. Honest and loving communication is very important in this step. Perhaps the most challenging part of marriage is when our partner brings a missed block to our attention. It takes only two words to lay such a block properly: "I'm sorry." Those are probably the hardest words to say without adding an excuse. But an excuse greatly weakens our apology.

Option #3—Criticism: We can grab the missed block and throw it at our spouse. Soon we have a real block-throwing war. This upsets the children very much. If this continues, the children will hardly stay within the family walls any longer than they have to. Moreover, if we are throwing blocks at each other, we cannot possibly be building a good wall.

Option #4—Grudges: There is one option left, and it is the worst one of all. We can grab the missed blocks and stuff them into our backpacks. That way we have plenty of blocks handy in case we have a quarrel again. How are we going to lay blocks when we are carrying such a burden? Let's take our blocks out of our pack and present them to our spouse, not to shift blame, but to apologize for having carried them. Then let us pray to Jesus to take them away—permanently.

As important as it is to use mortar on every block you lay, it is nevertheless impossible to build a wall with just mortar. Love without actions is a hollow shell. Too often a courtship is based on physical attraction. If you do not learn about true love and communication during courtship, the feelings you had will likely shatter at your feet after marriage.

When parents separate or go through a divorce, the children are thrown into an emotional turmoil that is tragic. The same is true when their parents live together in conflict—this is also very confusing and disturbing to them.

In the face of trials, a properly functioning family can deal with the problems that arise, and can use those problems as building blocks. Those same trials, however, can wreak havoc in a family that does not work together. Providing a loving, caring, and peaceful environment for our children is just as important as providing food and clothing to them.

—Author's name withheld, May 2004

Divorced at Heart

The Plain people do not accept divorce as an option. However, there are far too many of us living at the same address who are divorced at heart. My husband and I were on the verge of being one more couple in this sad state. We have been married for twenty-two years. Today we enjoy a happy, healthy, and godly marriage.

My husband got distracted by the cares of making a living. He did not take time to nurture our relationship, assuming that a good marriage just "happens." Some added stresses came along and both of us had needs that were not being met. Our marriage was in a mess. We were two hard and hurting people who showed up at church on the same buggy and gritted our teeth the rest of the week.

As John shut me out and threw himself into his work, I tried to "die to self." I thought I needed to submit more. I denied my pain. I blamed myself for even having needs. My heart finally turned to anger. My husband felt hurt by my unhappiness. He felt like a failure, and I was a constant reminder. It dragged on for years. I would have given up if it had not been for the children.

At last I went to the ministry. My husband was shocked and hurt that I ran to them without telling him. He felt betrayed, and it has been a long battle to regain his trust.

He has changed. He has learned to express warm and fond feelings, even though it does not come easily for him. He has learned to appreciate me as God's gift to help him, and he has learned he can meet my needs only by staying close to God.

I, too, have changed. I don't hold my feelings back until I am angry. I have learned to express myself to him calmly and as an adult. And I truly adore him! It is possible to overcome. Our marriage proves it.

—Happy and her husband, July 2006

Finding "Our Time"

After years of marriage, my husband and I still enjoy private talks with each other. These "dates" differ from the ones during our courtship. Our evenings back then were formal affairs.

The "dates" now are much more comfortable and relaxed. I know you young folks won't believe it of old married people like us, but they're more romantic, too. There is romance in the big, aromatic bouquets of wildflowers he brings me. My husband's hands are enchanting; muscular, work-worn hands engulfing his coffee cup.

The conversation of these special evenings has changed over the years. The talk has turned from the new song we sang at the singing and the upcoming weddings of friends to my relating cute things the children said or asking his advice on a behavior issue. My husband tells stories about his customers and expounds on soil science that he is studying. By the way, even the name of the special evenings has changed. No more "dates." Now we call it "our time."

So, my young friends, contrary to what you may believe, marriage doesn't get stodgy if you are willing to see that it doesn't! Sometimes life bogs you down; you suspect romance might, after all, be a thing of the past. But just try "our time."

Even if you turn out as I did—too plump and no stunning beauty—your husband won't mind, if you love him, no matter what. Young men, if you treat your wives as a godly man should, you need never worry if the hair on top of your head is disappearing like ice in the Sahara sun and the wedding suit has grown too tight. She remembers how handsome you looked when you came courting, but she thinks you are stunning now.

—Anonymous, January 2020

* * *

Amish Mothers

The following were selected to give an idea of typical days for Amish mothers, the roles they fill, and the challenges they face.

All in a Day's Work

My dream ends abruptly and my foggy brain fights to register as one of our twin babies demands her feeding. I fetch her and climb back into bed, doze off, wake up, and return her to her crib. I am almost asleep when loud cries from upstairs reach my ears. The two-year-old is coming down the stairs and is on her way to our bed. She has had a bad nightmare and is shaking all over as she crawls in, trying to get as close as possible.

Thirty minutes later Baby wakes again. Finally all is quiet and everyone is asleep. Toward morning another loud cry sounds and Baby's twin wakes up. I creep away from the two-year-old to tend to him and hope to get to sleep again. An hour later the five-year-old appears at the door, wondering where his little sister is. I try to make sleeping on the couch sound appealing, and finally he leaves and I sigh. What next?

Half an hour later he appears again, asking when he will get up. I tell him if he dresses he may go with Dad to the barn. He agrees, but is back within minutes and needs help with something. I groan my way out of bed, my head swimming. What a way to start the day!

My husband and the five-year-old leave for the barn, and I doze off on the rocker. Here comes the two-year-old, happy and chipper. She sees me, returns to the bedroom, and wakes her baby brother. I groan, fetch the baby, dress the two-year-old, and start with breakfast. Two-year-old thinks she did the right thing and returns to the bedroom to wake the second baby. I fetch the baby and plop her on the floor beside her brother. The babies are happy to see each other, and I feel better.

Dad comes in for breakfast, grabs a baby with each arm, and deposits them into high chairs. Breakfast begins; we salt and blow eggs for the older two and spoon cereal into the babies' mouths.

Breakfast is over and I make rounds with the washcloth, wiping dirty faces and hands. Dad picks up Twin Boy, dries him, and gags over the smell. I take him and Dad dresses Twin Girl, but she cries, so I plop Twin Boy down again and rescue her. I tell the five-year-old to clear the table, but he gets into a fight with the two-year-old, so Dad has to settle that.

I give toys to the twins and run out to start washing out diapers. Dad and the five-year-old leave, and when I return Twin Boy is crying and the two-year-old is trying to hold him, which makes him cry louder. I pick him up, put him in the walker, and start washing dishes quickly. I run to the barn with scraps, find a heifer loose, and run to tell Dad. On my return to the house, I hear loud cries in the kitchen. The baby on the floor had rolled over and the baby in the walker was trying to drive over her. I comfort the baby and take her to safety. I go back to the wash, hang up a load, and sweep the kitchen.

The two-year-old wants to go outside, so I put on her socks and shoes. Twin Boy wails faintly, the kitchen's empty, so where is he? I find him in the bedroom where the two-year-old had locked him in. I go back to the kitchen. The two babies are wailing, so I give them crackers, sink into a chair, and think, "It's time to start the day's work—what must be done first?" I have no time to decide, as I untangle Twin Boy's finger from Twin Girl's hair. He cries and she finds a toy to play with, but bumps her head on a sharp corner. I put Twin Boy on the floor and pick up and comfort Twin Girl. She goes to sleep, so I put her to bed and rock Twin Boy to sleep.

I look at the clock and gasp. It's almost time to start the noon meal. I hang up another load of wash and think of the sewing that should be done, but my sewing machine sits quietly in the repair shop. I enter the kitchen and hear the five-year-old in the bedroom, looking for me. He has pain so I try to soothe it.

I get the cookbook and page through it for an idea of what to bake. The two oldest children enter the kitchen, their boots and coats off, ready to play. I look at them, think of the warm weather, and send them back out. Alone in the kitchen, I sit down, and my head spins in the sudden silence. The door opens and the five-year-old is back in, wondering what they can play. I am low in ideas and even lower in patience. I order him out-side and start to mix a cake. The door opens and I send the children out again. I start dinner and hang up another load of wash.

I come back to the kitchen and sink into a chair to rest and regain patience. Dinner cooks, babies wake up, I fetch them, change them, and set them on the floor. I sit down beside them with a book in my hand. The babies smile at each other and at me, and I count my blessings.

—*A Mother of Preschoolers*, October 1995

What Am I?

> On the line for "occupation"
>> I'd write "homemaker"—
> When making bread and pies,
>> should I then write "baker"?
> Or when for a recipe I must look—
>> does mealtime turn me into a "cook"?
> Now the meal's over—
>> and it was delicious,
> Would I write "pot scrubber"
>> when I do the dishes?

There's dusting to do—
    the lamp looks shady,
Now what am I?
    A "cleaning lady"?
The crooked picture
    won't wait till later
As I fix it, maybe
    I'd write "decorator."
Or give medicine to a child
    that's worse,
Now tell me, am I a "doctor"
    or a "nurse"?
We've read the story
    and a picture made,
Am I now classed as
    a "teacher's aide"?
A seam is ripped so
    I'll fix the dress.
Would the paper have room
    for me as "seamstress"?
The toy wagon won't hitch,
    so I'll put on a hook,
can this get me in
    the "carpenter's" book?
The sun is out so the grass
    will really grow,
Does a "gardener" cut grass,
    or just use a hoe?
Now if I milk cows
    and give calves hay,
Do they know I was also
    a "farmer" today?
And so the time and

the days whiz by,
But the question remains—
Just what am I?
—Anonymous, August/September 1996

* * *

My Father's Guiding Influence

Dad was usually the one to get us up in the morning. He would come upstairs and go from room to room and light our lamps, telling us it was time to get up. I especially treasure the last several months that he lived. In the mornings he would sometimes pull up a chair beside my bed and just talk to me for a while. He was worried about me. He was worried about the direction my life seemed to be heading, and he was concerned about some of my attitudes.

He was also struggling with pressing issues outside of the family. He had been given a lot of responsibility in the church and community, and he took the responsibility seriously.

It was difficult for me to tell the difference between when he was saying something for my admonition and when he was unburdening his soul of his own struggles and fears. At those times there was no scolding or chastisement—he only shared his heart. There is no doubt in my mind that those early morning talks played a large part in turning my life around and making me what I am today.

In looking back at my childhood and teenage years, I can never remember a time when I got the feeling my father didn't trust me. When I betrayed his trust he was crushed, but not condemning. If I failed him in any way, I could tell that it broke his heart, but he was always ready to give me another try. His confidence in my integrity remained. How could I then go forth and be anything less than the son my father considered me to be?

It didn't matter whether it was to send us to town by ourselves at a comparatively young age or to go ahead with the work at home while Dad was on a trip. Because of his trust we generally proved faithful.

He didn't try to clear away all obstacles and temptations from our path. Rather, he strove to instill in us a conscience and an ability to deal with things as they came up.

Never do I recall that our parents openly disagreed in front of us children. Dad always considered Mom in his decisions, but he was the final authority, and we all knew it. Mom never stuck up for us; she always supported him, even though I now know she didn't always feel that way about it. I am convinced the fact that our parents had a strong marriage relationship went a long way toward giving us a good emotional foundation to build upon.

—Anonymous, August/September 1999

* * *

To My Single Friend

Today in church I saw you pick up our baby and hold him close. My heart went out to you because I knew what you were thinking. I knew you were trying to still the deep inner longing within your heart—the longing to have a husband and family and little babies to cuddle and love. You may wonder how I know. Because for many years I walked the single life, too, and I know how it feels.

Dear beloved single one, do not despair. Your life can be a great blessing, if in God's will you make it so. Your school teaching job puts you in a position to influence hundreds of young people. You are a key factor in molding their lives, in helping them form good habits, in teaching them self-discipline, in preparing their souls for eternity. These young people are our future churches and communities.

Later in the afternoon, I saw you take your aged, widowed mother by the arm and lead her gently out the door. You helped her on the buggy, and then the two of you drove away together. Your mother depends on you for so many things. You are a great comfort to her since she has parted from her life companion. How thankful she must be for you—her single daughter.

May God be your companion and help you in your work. You will be richly rewarded if it is done in submission and unselfishness and love. May God bless all our single sisters!

Lovingly, Your Married Friend

—Anonymous, November 1993

* * *

Forming a Family by Adoption

It is very true that if we cannot be happy and content *without* children, neither will we be happy and content *with* children.

After seven years of marriage, we were privileged to become parents, but to children not born biologically to us. They became ours through the joy and responsibility of adoption. There is more than one way to build a family and to fill those empty arms. It can be done through foster care or adopting.

If you are considering adoption, please work through the grief of infertility before you adopt. A child should be adopted for what you can do for him or her, and not for what the child can do for you. Having said that, let me add that loving a child fills a space in your heart as nothing else will.

—Mervin and Janice Hoover, July 2015

Blessings in Adoption

What a wonderful blessing it is when people open their hearts and homes to the orphaned and homeless. They love the dear little children so much that they are willing to reach out and take them under their wings as one of their own. They give them lots of love, a home, a family, and wholesome food, and most of all, they give them a chance to know about God.

While there are many homeless children, others grow up in abusive homes. Some are starving from hunger, and some are starving for tender loving care. Some live with drug-addicted parents who think more of their drugs than of their precious children. Some children get shuffled from home to home because nobody really wants them, or because their parents are in prison.

I myself am adopted, and my husband and I have adopted our family. So I have experienced the blessings both ways. It is so precious and worth the efforts and trials. I have met with my biological mother, and she said it is a great blessing that I was adopted into a Christian home. She told me, "Don't ever decide to leave your way of living. You have too much to lose. The world out here has nothing to offer. It is full of hatred, drugs, alcohol, cheating and stealing, divorce and remarriage over and over."

I am so grateful for my father and mother who opened their hearts and home and loved me as their own flesh and blood. Everybody has a desire to be loved. Nobody has any control over the kind of home he was born into. I wish God's blessings to the couples who have pursued and completed adoptions. If it were not for unselfish and caring people like you, where would I be now?

—*Richly Blessed by Adoption*, July 2007

* * *

Recipe for Sunday Morning at Home (with Sick Child or Mother)

1 exhausted wife
1 patient husband
2 or more energetic children

Take husband out of bed when first child wakes up. Place him and child in kitchen, where he fixes breakfast. Return him to bedroom to fetch other children when they awaken. Return him to kitchen to set table, then to bedroom to fetch his sheepish wife, who didn't realize how late it is!

Best if used only once or twice a year.

—*A Thankful Wife*, October 1994

FIVE

The Young

FAMILY MEANS CHILDREN. No matter who you are or where you live, raising a family and helping your children navigate the changing, often turbulent waters of the world is challenging but important work: every society recognizes its young as its future. But some children experience a disconnect when they receive mixed messages between their life at home, at school, at church, in the media, and with peers. In the Amish world, these realms are more integrated, especially with the preservation of the one-room schoolhouse. But that does not mean parents find it easy to raise a family. The topic of discipline can be controversial...too strict or too liberal? "Losing" children to the modern world is also a real concern, and can be traumatic for parent and child. Yet in many ways, the Amish prepare their young to be successful and stable contributing members of society.

Over the past fifty years of the magazine, many of the same challenges, concerns, and pleas for advice have continued. In these selections, one often finds the most heartfelt and honest words anywhere in the publication. Emotions can sometimes be raw. Each member and family is different, with their own set of circumstances. It is fascinating to read these reflections on teaching and learning from each other, mistakes made, and suggested guidelines to follow.

Parenting

No Better Than Adam

"There is a sale over in Auburn, and I'd like to go," Dad said as the family sat down to eat. When the meal was over, the plates were taken away and Dad read to the family. That morning Dad read from the third chapter of Romans [verse 23—"All have sinned, and come short of the glory of God"]. When he was finished he asked the children questions about it to see how well they understood. He also gave the children the chance to ask questions.

"Dad," said Michael, "what did it mean about all coming short?"

"It means that we are all sinners at heart," Dad explained. "None of us can do any good without God. If given the choice, we humans always choose to do the selfish thing. However, with God's help we can overcome that part of ourselves."

"But, Dad, you teach us not to be selfish. I mean, we'd get into trouble if we act too selfishly. We all know it's wrong." Robert was truly puzzled.

"That's just it, son." Dad said. "Even if we know it's wrong, we sometimes do it anyway. Just like Adam and Eve, for example. They knew what they did was against God's commandment, but they did it anyway."

After breakfast, the rest of the family prepared to go to the sale. As he got into the surrey, Dad gave Robert and Michael some final instructions.

"And one more thing. I left a box on the kitchen counter. You may do whatever you please today, except *don't* look into that box." With that he signaled to the horse, and they rode away.

Mentally, Robert planned the long afternoon ahead of them. They had no work to do. They could do just what they wanted. Then he saw that box again. He felt as if he were not really able to enjoy his freedom with that mysterious box sitting there tempting him. He picked it up. It was light.

"Why, there is nothing in it," he muttered. Now he was more curious than ever. He shook the box. He was positive it was empty.

Then Robert couldn't stand it any longer. He opened the box. At first he thought it was indeed empty, but then he saw a piece of paper taped to the bottom. He squinted to read it. The words were clearly in Dad's handwriting. It took Robert a few seconds to get it, but then he realized the message was for him. Dad had actually expected him to open the box. He read the words again:

You are no better than Adam. (We all need Jesus.) —Dad

Robert had to smile despite himself. Even though he knew he had failed the test Dad had set up for him, he didn't feel overly sad or disappointed. He felt human, just like everyone else.

—Anonymous, November 2004

A Memo from Your Child

1. Don't spoil me. I know quite well that I ought not to have everything I ask for. I am only testing you when I ask.

2. Don't be afraid to be firm with me. I prefer this, for it makes me feel more secure.

3. Don't let me form bad habits. I am relying on you to detect them in their early stages.

4. Don't make me feel smaller than I am. It only makes me act "stupidly" big.

5. Don't correct me in front of others, if you can help it. I take much more notice if you do it in private.

6. Don't make me feel that my mistakes are sinful. This upsets my sense of values.

7. Don't protect me from everyday consequences. I need to learn the painful way at times.

8. Don't take too much notice of my small ailments. Sometimes I use them to get the attention I want.

9. Don't nag, please. I shall have to protect myself by appearing as if I'm deaf.

10. Don't make rash promises. Remember, I feel badly let down if a promise is broken.

11. Don't be inconsistent. That completely confuses me and makes me lose confidence in you.

12. Don't put me off when I ask questions. If you do, you will find that I'll seek information elsewhere.

13. Don't tell me my fears are silly. They are terribly real to me, and I like it when you reassure me, understandingly.

14. Don't ever suggest you are perfect or infallible. It gives me a terrible shock when I discover you aren't.

15. Don't be afraid to apologize to me. An honest apology builds respect toward you.

16. Don't forget how quickly I am growing up. Otherwise, it will be very difficult for you.

17. Don't forget that I cannot thrive without lots of understanding love. But I don't have to tell you, do I?

—*Your child*, October 2006

Discipline at the Table

The table for us as Plain people is in many ways as the family altar. Around it we gather at a set time, and we often plan our schedule according to that time. Around the table we have many discussions about our home life, about school activities, and community happenings. We have devotions; we read and sing and pray.

First we bow our heads, close our eyes, and fold our hands on our laps. We ask God to bless this food to the nourishment of our body, so that we can better serve him. We ask him to bless the food so that we can go about our daily duties with a vigor. If we then commence to eat and say, "I don't like this or I don't care for that," we are rejecting the food we have just finished asking God to bless.

We would consider it wasteful to leave food on our plates, especially if we think of the many thousands of hungry children in the world. To allow a child to eat only what he wants is not training him to be thankful or appreciative. Neither is it teaching him to be submissive. Rather, he is being allowed to please himself. This can be labeled as selfishness.

—William Yutzy, February 2020

* * *

"Mother, what could I do next?" asked five-year-old Violet as she neatly hung up the tea towel.

"I've been thinking," answered Mother thoughtfully, "that we should send a letter to your grandmother. She is going to a hospital far away, you know."

"Will you help me write a letter?" Violet bounced up and down in excitement.

"Yes, I will help you." Mother's eyes twinkled. She brought paper and pencil to the table. Together they worked long and hard. This is what the letter said:

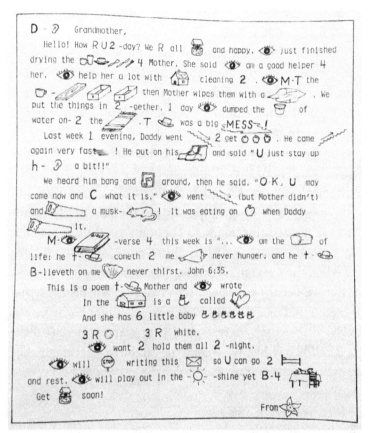

—Anonymous, March 1994

* * *

Guidelines for Parents

The following selection includes excerpts from talks given by various Amish ministers on the subject of parenting and child training that were published in *Family Life* magazine over the course of a few months.

1. Being worthy of your child's respect

To develop a good relationship with our children and to encourage their respect, discipline is necessary. Children want to know what they may and may not do. They want to know where the boundaries are.

The second thing I want to mention is being consistent. Children lose their respect and confidence if parents are not consistent, or if they ask the children to do things they themselves wouldn't do. I think of a saying I heard: "An ounce of walk is worth more than a ton of talk."

The third thing I would like to touch on is the need to give praise. We all need that. But for children it is a must. It is very important to give praise and not just criticism.

I have to think of the puppy we got for the farm last summer. We wanted this puppy to become a good farm dog. But first we had to choose a name to suit everyone. Not everyone agreed on the name to give to our new puppy.

But we needn't have worried. With so many people trying to train him, I'm afraid that little puppy thought his name was "NO!" That doesn't make a good puppy, and it doesn't make good children either. We want to be careful to respect our children's feelings, too, if we expect them to respect us.

2. Right motives in child training

The dictionary defines *motive* as something that moves a person to action. If we have wrong motives, things will not hold up. The primary wrong motive that came to my mind is being too concerned about what others think instead of what God in heaven wants of us.

When parents work together, much can be achieved. Father and Mother must share the same vision, work toward the same goals, support each other in love and unity. Here is a little story that may illustrate this truth . . .

Two boys were walking down the street. Up ahead they noticed people trying to move a piano through a doorway. They saw they were having trouble, so they stopped to help. They all shoved and shoved, but they just couldn't move it. They knew the piano was heavy, but they didn't think it was that heavy.

Finally one of the boys said, "We might as well give up. It's too heavy! We'll never get this piano in."

The ones on the inside were astonished. "In!" they exclaimed. "We aren't trying to get it in. We want to get it out!"

The world today admits, even proudly, that they are the *now* generation. They don't concern themselves about the generation before or what may come after them. They put their parents in a nursing home and their children in the daycare center. That is not what the Scriptures teach. We are to look beyond the present moment, both back into the past and forward into the future. We can see our parents' mistakes. They are already made. But it would be sad if we couldn't learn from the mistakes our parents made.

3. Work ethics in the home
How can we as parents get our children to be a help? (1) Take time to teach our children how to do things. Give them pointers. (2) Never take for granted that your children already know how to do something. (3) Develop a habit of speaking aloud while you are working with them, explaining why and how you do things.

4. Emotional security for our children
Unless by the grace of God we can forgive others and teach our children to do the same, they will go through life emotionally crippled. We need to develop and teach the attitude of loving our neighbor, faults and all.

By putting others down, we are exalting ourselves. We need to teach our children to suffer reproach without feeling sorry for themselves.

Another thing that causes emotional damage is the anger of parents. If we discipline in anger, we provoke more anger. It is more the attitude we have when we discipline our children than the method we use.

A father's thoughtfulness will show up again in his children. If Dad is gentle and respects Mom, it will set the tone for the children. No amount of talking will bring results as effectively as will our example. To give a child good instruction and a bad example is like telling him to walk on the way to heaven and leading him by the hand on the way to hell.

5. The needs of our children

Children can slow us down in our work. We could often do a job faster by ourselves. But the children get a good feeling of being involved if they can help. They will feel that they belong, that they are a part of the family.

There's a little story of a father who was polishing his car. His little boy was watching him. Finally he said, "Daddy, this car is worth a lot, isn't it?"

His father answered, "Yes, it cost a lot, and if I take good care of it, it will be worth more when I sell it again."

The little fellow didn't say anything for a while. Then he said, "Daddy, I'm not worth much, am I?" You see, he didn't think his dad spent much time with him. We may be busy and pressed down, but let's spend time with our children.

We all make mistakes. Children will learn with time that we are not perfect. Apologizing for our mistakes will build up respect, not tear it down.

6. Husband and wife relationships

A person could speak for a long time on this topic and still not be done. On the other hand, this question can be answered in a few simple words. Just one short paragraph, and I can take my seat . . .

"Husband and wife must be in God's order to receive his blessings in their marriage and in the home."

God intended that there be one man and one woman, and *the two shall be one*. Mothers have one of the greatest and most far-reaching assignments of anyone in the whole world—to love their husbands and their children, and at the same time stay in their God-given order.

I came across a statement that made a profound impression on me: "The greatest thing a father can do for the welfare of his children is to love their mother." That is in perfect accord with what the Bible teaches us: "Husbands, love your wives, even as Christ loved the church and died for it."

7. *Shaping the will of a child*

I would like to focus mainly on the early years, with special emphasis on *bonding*—a bond of love. Bonding ties together, it holds together. Bonding in love is the foundation and cornerstone of child training.

Bonding comes naturally for mothers, but not so easily for us fathers. To form bonds of love between the child and the father, the father must take an effort and spend time with the child from babyhood.

Parents leave an influence by their daily example—in community service, honesty in business dealings, promptness at mealtimes, punctuality, and so on. We also teach by example in how we manage our anger, if we have respect for others, and whether temporal values or eternal values are most important to us. Indeed, in all these ways we parents shape the will of our children.

—Anonymous, excerpts from April, May, and June 2002

* * *

Growing Up

Teen Commandments

1. Don't let your parents down; they brought you up.
2. Choose your companions with care; you become what they are.
3. Be master of your habits or they will master you.
4. Treasure your time; don't spend it, invest it.
5. Stand for something or you'll fall for anything.
6. If you are too busy to pray, you are busier than God wants you to be.
7. See what you can do for others, not what others can do for you.
8. Guard your thoughts. What you think, you are.
9. Don't fill up on the world's crumbs; feed your soul on the Living Bread.
10. Give your all to Christ; he gave his all for you.

—Karen Kilmer, March 1994

I Am a Builder

My daddy is a builder—
He makes things big and small,
And I can be a builder too,
But not that kind at all.

When Daddy builds, he uses nails,
A hammer, saw, and wood,
And I use truth and kindness,
And habits that are good.

I'll try to do that which is right,
Say no to what is wrong,
And keep in mind the golden rule,
To practice all day long.

For when I build my character,
I should do all I can.
My dad can build a house or barn,
But I must build a man.

—E. M. G., February 1997

A Letter to My Parents

Do you realize what a big responsibility you are placing on my shoulders when you send me out into a worldly workplace environment? The influences I am under will greatly affect the rest of my life. After all, I am just a teenager yet.

I might not have told you much about my job, Dad and Mom, but you can judge for yourself. Is my employer a Christian? Is he of our faith? Are you aware that a steady diet of profane and loose laughing is being poured daily into my ears? Do you know that I have easy access to the radio and TV? I don't mean to condemn every workplace out there, Dad and Mom. I'm just asking some questions.

In a way it hurts me, Dad and Mom, that you show such little concern. You just took it calmly in stride when my brother told you at the supper table that I drive the boss's truck at work. I watched your expression closely as you heard it. Mom, you only gave me a reproving look, and you, Dad, you grinned. I know you love me and want the best for me. Something inside of me twisted up into a terrible knot just then.

Do you know that my coworkers scoff and deride the faith you have? Do you realize how dangerous it is for me to hear all those confusing things when I have not yet committed my life to God? Do you know I feel like I'm on a little boat, and every day my coworkers push me further and further from shore? The little pull I get in the evening from you at home, Dad and Mom, just isn't enough. It won't keep me near the harbor.

You don't like it that I'm becoming loud and bold. You tried to shame me into being quieter and more reserved. But don't you remember how our dog, Bandit, was spoiled by running around with that stray? We fed Bandit, gave him a home, controlled, and punished him. Still, in the end the stray's bad company ruined him.

Fine, Dad and Mom. I'll keep this job. You've told me you need the money. You'll weep when I stop going to church. You will beg for me to wear my plain clothes. You'll sorrowfully tell other people you did the best you knew in raising me. Other people will nod their heads and agree.

But, Dad and Mom, I know better. I will know how it really was. I am, Your son.

—Anonymous, June 2009

* * *

Youth Groups

A question from a young adult concerning how to establish and conduct youth groups—the social gatherings for a community's teenagers—resulted in many replies, showing the variety of activities (and opinions) in different Amish communities.

Youth, along with some of the parents, can get together to sing. Young people can help the elderly, widows, sick, or other struggling people with their work. The growing practice of families and young people playing, camping, and sightseeing does not contribute to the spiritual growth of those involved.

—Lehman Martin, December 2010

The advantage of written guidelines is that the youth know what is expected of them. This creates a feeling of security. The committee, kindly with love, should remind them of their limits and discipline violations. They should do this with the spirit of servants and caretakers, and not as dictators.

In our community this was started as very small groups with standards already established, thus giving a young person the choice to abide by them or leave the group. After the groups grew, they were divided by area.

Sunday afternoons are spent playing volleyball, quoits, or croquet or visiting. Volleyball is the most popular, and has the advantage of more young people participating in one game.

Evening singings are held at the same place as supper, and start at seven o'clock or shortly thereafter. The only activity afterward is a limited time for a snack and visiting around the table.

The support of our bishops and ministers is the backbone of our supervised groups with standards based on church *Ordnung*. The foremost regret for me is that we did not have such an opportunity when we were young.

—*A Lancaster County parent*, December 2010

We have been blessed to be a part of a church that cares about its youth. Our ministers realized that youth have energy, and that we as a church are responsible to make use of that in a godly way. At the start of the new year, twelve families each choose a month in which they are willing to take responsibility for the youth.

During that month, we try to have a work evening to help someone, and then also one evening is set aside for volleyball, or a similar activity. And then every third Sunday of that month is set aside for meetings in homes for people of the community, with the youth taking part, and then we usually have the young people come to our house for lunch or supper. Our young people need to know they are needed and that we appreciate them.

—*Appreciating our youth*, December 2010

* * *

When Children Walk Away

Although 85 percent or more of young people decide to be baptized and become Amish, there are those who do not. As with parents anywhere, Amish are saddened when a child decides not to join the faith. Some "Broken-Hearted Parents" wrote with a request for advice: "We are greatly saddened by the path our wayward children have taken. Those of you who have had this experience, how did you cope with it? Did they return? If so, what helped to bring that about? Should they be asked to stop coming home if they come with stylish clothes and cars? What is the reason such children leave us? It is so painful and so many people do not understand."

There may be a number of different reasons as to why children leave us. A few of the main ones may be: (1) The strong peer pressure among some youth groups may cause many to become tangled in the web of rebellion and worldliness. They choose the world with its false promise of pleasure, not discerning that it leads to bondage. (2) Broken relationships have caused many to become discouraged. Restored relationships have often done wonders to draw them back to the fold. (3) A poor workplace environment cannot help but affect those who are exposed to it day after day, rubbing shoulders with ungodly people.

To those of you who have not experienced disobedient children, be thankful and please be charitable in your judgments. For hurting people, it is difficult enough to face the community without the burden of knowing that careless gossip is making its rounds.

—*With love for all*, October 2004

Our son came home after spending two years out in the world. Fourteen months later he left again. What brought him home? He said he missed us. We can see that it has to go deeper than this if a change is to last.

About letting your children come home with their fancy clothes and fine cars, our feelings are . . . no, if you want to show the rest of the family you do not approve of their waywardness.

—*Praying for a change of heart*, October 2004

Our wayward children weighed heavily on our hearts. It is so hard to see them willfully turn their backs on us, feeling they know better and just do as they please.

We told our children, "We want to live for God, and that is the way we tried to bring you up. Cars, worldly clothes, radios, smoking, will not go. If you insist on these things, you must seek a home somewhere else. Our door is always open for you to come home if you wish to live a godly life and be one of us. But not like this."

The choice was theirs. They left. Then they were no longer included in family affairs until they returned. Later, they admitted the world has nothing satisfying to offer. These hard knocks helped draw us closer to God. There alone did we find true comfort.

—Anonymous, October 2004

By the grace of God, ours all came back. Our children are now all married but one. When we have our family night and they all come home with their children whom they are raising up in the nurture and admonition of the Lord, then I just send up a silent thank you again to God for all his blessings to us.

—*Understanding friends in Indiana*, October 2004

* * *

Johnny and His Father

Dear little boy with eyes so blue,
Those eyes that beg and shine,
Says, "Daddy, would you help me search
For that old ball of mine?
I've lost it and I just don't know
Where that ball might be found.
It could be in this box of toys,
Or out upon the ground."

"Well, Johnny, I am busy now,
I have no time to find it.
I must go out and feed the cows,
I hope you do not mind it.
There's hay to cut, a fence to mend,
And cornfields need attention.
Then there are many other tasks—
Lots more than I can mention."

"Where are you going now, my son?
Why don't you stay tonight?
We'd like to see you home some more,
But seems you just delight
In always being with your friends.
But why not come and sit;
We'll play a game and pop some corn,
And talk and sing a bit?"

"Well, Father, I am busy now,
I really cannot bother.
The fellows will be here just soon—
Mark told us to come over.
I'd rather be there with the guys
Than sitting here and playing.
I'm really quite grown up by now,
So guess I won't be staying."

"Now, John, it seems like quite a while
Since you've been here to see me.
I'd like to hold my new grandson
While he is still a baby.
Just bring the children over, please,
And spend an hour or two.
It sure would mean so much to me
To have some time with you."

"Well, Father, I am busy now,
There's always work to do.
Don't know when we'll have time to come
To sit around with you.
I've all these bills that I must pay,
Plus other things to do.
And so I'm working hard each day,
Just as you taught me to!"

—Anonymous, February 2005

SIX

Work

IF THERE IS ONE THING that has been constant in the pages of *Family Life* over the past fifty years, it is the continuing discussion about farm versus "factory" (nonfarm) work. Farmland scarcity and prices have driven Amish farmers to other states. Farmers have also changed some of their practices. As milk prices fell, some sold their cows. Others found success in growing vegetables. Those who wanted to stay on the farm shared their problems and solutions in the magazine.

But these changes in farming also meant that many decided to work in nonfarm occupations. Some even worked in factories. The Amish refer to the "lunch bucket problem," meaning Dad left home to work and was not seen again until the evening. Over time, the rise of cottage industries meant more Amish could work at home—making furniture or running a store, for example. Working locally for other Amish people limited exposure to the influences of the outside world. But it also meant adopting the use of some modern technology to stay competitive in business. Yes, some Amish businesses have websites, or at least pay someone to maintain them, right down to email exchanges. Some Amish businesses gross a million dollars or more. But the farmer's life has not changed to such a major degree.

And so the debate continues. Is one way of life better than the other? What are the plusses and minuses to each? Is one more "Amish" than the other? Is Amish "big business" bad? Is farming idealized too much? Are people not willing to sacrifice and work as hard as they used to? (My Amish friend once said the greatest threat to the Amish was prosperity.) I have found this back-and-forth fascinating, and I hope you do, too, while also seeing some of the joys and advantages of both ways of life within the Amish world.

Amish Farming: Past, Present, and Future

Although the Anabaptist movement had its beginnings among educated city dwellers, it soon spread to the rural areas of Switzerland. To avoid persecution, many people also left the cities and fled to remote parts of the country to evade the authorities. Former merchants, tailors, and cobblers were suddenly farmers. At that time, it was mostly a subsistence type of farming.

In areas where persecution lessened, the Anabaptists became excellent farmers. In some instances, they led to the development of new techniques that improved productivity. Second, they were even invited to move to certain areas by friendly rulers who saw their farming abilities.

Despite their skills, few of our ancestors actually owned the land they farmed. Throughout much of Europe, those who did not belong to the state church could only be tenants or caretakers of estates. America offered not only freedom of religion, but also the opportunity to possess their own farms. Therefore, many families forsook the homeland and moved to the United States and Canada. With lots of hard work and many hardships, they established homes, communities, and churches.

They could now build their own barns, plow their own fields, and tend their own livestock.

When the Amish arrived in America, farmwork was still mostly done by hand. Hay and grain were cut with scythes. The gathering and loading onto wagons was all done by hand. So was the threshing and putting the crops into the barn. Oxen supplied most of the power in the field. Before 1800, horses were used very little for farming.

Soon after the Amish came, major changes took place in agriculture. The 1800s could well be called the century of machinery. The steel moldboard plow, harrow, disc and packer, grain drill, and later the corn planter and harvesting machinery all came into widespread use. Farming became increasingly mechanized. All this machinery was pulled by horses.

Up to [about] 1900, most Amish accepted all these farm improvements. In fact, some of our people were involved in fine-tuning equipment, or they were the first in the area to use a machine. Time-saving farming methods greatly reduced the number of American people living on farms, from 97 percent in 1863 to only 36 percent in 1900.

In the late 1800s, most people had their own dairy cow, even those who lived in a city. With the Industrial Revolution, many cows in town were sold, thus forming a market for dairy products. Farms with good pasture sold for a premium, and dairy cattle became the leading livestock enterprise on the nation's farms.

At the turn of the century, the first automobiles appeared, mostly in cities since country roads were not suitable for such vehicles. By 1910, country roads were graveled, which brought the automobiles to rural areas, but the Amish chose not to accept them, fearing the effect of such unrestrained mobility.

Tractors were invented. If a motor could drive a carriage, why couldn't it also drive a plow? The first tractors were basically motors set onto plows, propelled with a big drive wheel. These clumsy, unwieldy machines were not practical for small farms. As the design improved, Amish farmers were faced with the decision whether or not to make use of them. After accepting a host of labor-saving horse-drawn machinery in the past decades, they drew the line at the tractor. And to keep horses in the field would help maintain horses as a means of transportation.

Huge steam engines had been used for some years for threshing, sawmills, and grinding feed. When tractors came along, they largely replaced the steam engine for belt power. Even though the tractor provided stationary power around the barn, it was not permitted for field use.

By studying general farm literature from the 1920s, it is obvious that the Amish have basically adopted the methods of that era and have maintained them for many years. A crop rotation of hay, corn, and small grains was advocated. Silos were strongly promoted as an important feature of the farm. This was a defining era in Amish history. When they did not accept the automobile, the tractor, and electricity, the Amish were identified as a separate people.

The United States had barely recovered from the Depression when it was thrown into World War II, and all factories turned to producing war machinery. But after the war, wheat prices remained strong and the cost of production low. Amish farmers had the advantage of buying horse-drawn machinery very cheaply from those who had switched to tractor farming. They were able to buy farms for their children, too.

After 1960, wheat prices dropped considerably, driven down by western farmers with combines who could now cover vast acreages. These big-time farmers also received subsidies and low-interest government loans, which the Amish chose not to accept. It became impractical to grow wheat on small acreages at such low prices. This was the first indication of the squeeze that Amish farmers would soon face.

Now that wheat was no longer a viable cash crop, Amish farmers focused on dairy. They grew more corn and milked more cows. The hog market had its highs and lows but still provided a decent supplemental income.

By the 1960s, good horse-drawn equipment was becoming hard to find. Some more mechanically inclined farmers built new equipment, or they made replacement parts for older machinery. This grew, for some, into a full-time occupation, and thus the Amish shop was born.

The number of available farms in the larger Amish settlements had decreased while the prospects of other high-paying jobs had increased. Many "English" sold their farms to their Amish neighbors, and there were now large areas where all the farms were owned by our people. As children married, instead of moving farther out and staying in agriculture, many built houses on the corners of the farm and worked as carpenters or in some shop.

After 1970, the larger communities expanded very little geographically, but experienced tremendous internal development and growth. Land prices climbed. The younger generation could hardly dream of farming unless they could buy the home farm at below-market value.

By the 1980s, some farms stood practically idle while their owners worked off the farm. Others tried to stay successful by milking more cows and farming the neighbors' fields. Farmers were nearly overwhelmed by the workload of growing more and more feed to produce more and more milk. This brought pressure to have more labor-saving equipment.

Under these conditions, only a small percentage of farmers thrived financially. The majority struggled. During the 1990s, the biggest mortgage lifter was income from children's jobs off the farm. The younger generation had little incentive to pursue an agricultural livelihood.

In the United States, dairy herds with thirty to fifty cows have been largely eliminated. Thousands and thousands of small farmers have quit in the past fifty years. Apparently, modern equipment is not the solution.

Within the past ten years, there has been a major shift in Amish farming. To provide employment for their children at home, some families have diversified into other enterprises besides dairying. Niche markets [such as organic and produce] have been developed. Intensive rotational grazing has also made it much easier to produce milk for the organic market. Any farmer must be willing to put in a lot of effort to succeed.

—*A young Amish farmer*, June 2010

Do the Same for Someone Else

One of the main reasons we enjoy farming this way is the privilege of being at home and working with our family, seeing them grow and develop, and at the same time being close to nature. And the children can be given personal responsibilities at an early age, helping with chores and feeding certain animals.

Another strong point for this type of life is that the farmer is close to his investment. In comparison, the day laborer carries his assets home in his pocket at the end of the day. He is under greater temptation to spend it on unnecessary items at the grocery store or at Walmart. Money spent in such a way is gone forever—it ceases to be of any value to him.

In conclusion, maybe the greatest dividends that come from family-size general farming are the ones which don't show up in the income, things such as working together as a neighborhood in times of harvest.

And though our farm is paid for, we have not planned any expansion, as we want to make our profit available, interest free, to some other beginner. In fact, those were the terms the elderly couple who financed our farm specified—that we do the same for someone else.

—Anonymous, June 1994

Those Four and Twenty Feet

The sun is rising swiftly
    as I head out to the barn—
All the cows are milked,
    and the morning chores are done.
The horses nicker softly
    as I enter at the door,
"Oh, no, big boys," I tell them,
    "I didn't come to chore."

Mark lumbers over slowly
    to get his morning drink,
And once he hears he has to work
    he takes his time, I think.
Next in line is young horse Chief,
    so "Mark, I'll brush you now."
I finally get them harnessed
    and lead them to the plow.

"Mark and Nap, you come up front,
    I'll put you in the lead,
And, Chief, you too, here on the side,
    it's time you earn your feed."
Next I hook the three behind
    and climb up on the seat.
Then we head out toward the field
    with four and twenty feet.

Now I admit if you want speed,
    big tractors got them beat,
But I can say that I enjoy
    these four and twenty feet.

                —Roy Miller Jr., July 1995

Our Experience Growing Vegetables

After our marriage, my wife and I rented a farm for six years until a property close by came up for sale. We had to borrow all the money to buy our farm, and we had a tough time getting the funds until some friends helped us out by extending a loan for the final 25 percent of the purchase price.

I had in mind to work a part-time job off the farm. One of our creditors told us that if I did, something would suffer—either my job, my cows, my wife, or myself. Well, I tried it anyway, but to this day I think he gave me a pretty good piece of advice.

Five years later we were having serious doubts about farming. True, we had been making our payments, but our overall debt was just as high, if not higher than it had been when we bought the farm.

I enjoyed working in the garden, and in 1989 we planted some extra sweet corn and sold it out by the road in front of our house, piled on our little wagon. Each year we planted a few more vegetables to sell. By 1994 we were ready to go into it full-time and sold our cows.

I would say one of the biggest advantages of produce growing is that a person can get started with a minimum of investment. It is something that single boys and girls can do and have a nice profit, if managed right and the weather is good. One can start in slowly as a sideline, for it is usually not hard to sell a few dozen ears of corn, some baskets of fresh tomatoes, or pickling cucumbers from one's front yard.

Quality is the number one requirement, always spelled with a capital *Q*! Put yourself in the buyer's shoes and go on an imaginary tour to different vegetable stands. The ones with piles of fresh, good-looking vegetables arranged on a clean, orderly counter will surely attract repeat customers.

Some of our regular customers we know by name, but others we identify in various ways. The "Hot Pepper Dawdy" buys lots of hot peppers from us, and likes to show off how he can eat them raw. One time he misjudged and quickly had to eat a tomato to cool his mouth.

Another customer we refer to as "Beefsteak" because of his preference in [beefsteak] tomatoes, and also because he is well-rounded in his figure.

—John J. Byler, February 1999

Back to the Future: Our Roots in the Soil

Maybe the biggest mistake we make is to think of farming as a business instead of as a way of life. The modern view is exactly that—farming is a business and a fiercely competitive one at that. But perhaps we need to step back and take a broader look.

We need to go back and start all over. But what do we mean by back to the future? Does it mean going back two hundred years?

No, we are looking for principles that go back to the beginning for their base—back to the Word of God in the Bible and the laws of God in nature. These are the principles we must follow as we choose occupations for our people.

In no way would I undertake to explain what all these principles for a caring and sharing community are, but if we can touch on a few of them, maybe we can get our thoughts working.

1. Content with the basic needs.

2. Stewardship of natural resources.

3. Working with our hands.

4. Grow what we eat and eat what we grow.

Besides the above principles, our occupation ought to be honest, upbuilding, worthwhile, and good for our own welfare. It must also be good for our family, something we can do with our children, keeping us close to them so we can teach and train them in the ways of righteousness. Next, it should be something good for the community, a work that is needful and practical. I may need to give my own personal opinion of how an ideal caring and sharing community can be sustained.

In this ideal community, we need not all be dairy farmers. But it would be good if most families had a family cow. Neither would we even need to all be livestock farmers, although to me, a farm without livestock does not seem complete. Neither would we all want to be vegetable growers. But each family should have a garden, and everyone needs to once in a while get down on his hands and knees and dig in the dirt.

We need some carpenters to build our homes, sawmills to cut the lumber from our woodlots, furniture shops to make our furniture. But throughout the community as a whole, farming still needs to be the foundation.

Do we really need to understand the principles our customs and practices are based on? Can't we just pass these customs down from generation to generation without knowing why we do things a certain way? There are two dangers that can come with hand-me-down customs. If we do not base our practices on principles that we understand, we may slowly but surely be influenced by the pressures of the surrounding society. Or we can slip into the rut of formalism, so that the outward expression has no real meaning.

Time, places, and circumstances do bring changes. But the principles do not change. Each generation needs to understand the principles and be responsible to live by them, regardless of the circumstances. If we understand the values behind the principles, we can pass them on to our children—with conviction and meaning.

—*"Uncle Elmer,"* April 1997

Farm Life: Keeping Up with Its Changes

If our young people are to succeed on farms, not only will they have to think outside the box, but we older ones will have to as well. In a way, though, it may only be backing up in some things, going back to a system which was more cooperative.

We need to look back at those things that are causing our problem before we can see the solution. The problems are high land prices, which require high payments. Coupled with low commodity prices, which require high volumes. And made worse by the shortage of affordable hired help, which means that most families have to do it pretty much on their own. Any changes that don't address at least one of these problems is a step in the wrong direction.

Unless we make some changes in our attitude, we may be seeing the sun setting on our culture. Our population is doubling every eighteen to twenty years, which means we have to reproduce everything we have in that time period. Every community, every church, every school, and every farm. If the total number of Amish farms remains the same, then the percentage of the community who are farmers is halved every eighteen years. At that rate, it will take only another fifty years in some communities until only 2 percent of us will be farmers. That is the same as in the American population as a whole. If that isn't where we want to go, we will have to very consciously do something about it. And soon.

—Robert Alexander, excerpts from May and August/
September 2016

Farming Is Not All Roses

All we farmers' wives hear is how nice we have it with our husbands at home to help us and to babysit when we want to go away. But I've had it both ways, and I find that the workload for the wife on the farm is much greater.

Let me explain. When we didn't farm, once it was time to plant the garden, we'd have an early supper as soon as Daddy came home from work; then we'd all go out to the garden. He did the tilling and made the rows. Mom and the children did the planting. Then we all enjoyed a snack together afterward.

When the buggy needed washing, we'd do it together, or he'd do it while I mowed the yard or did other outside work. When I had canning, he helped me more than one evening or on Saturday. On Saturday we'd have a leisurely breakfast together. Then he'd go get groceries and do our banking while I did the Saturday cleaning. We shared a closeness from helping each other.

Now the other side. Since we are farming, the garden is mine. The children and I do it all. The lawn is my responsibility too. The buggy doesn't get washed unless I do it. On Saturday, I am the one who goes to do the banking, buys the groceries, not to mention the times during the week when I'll run and get parts for the hay mower or the baler. All this plus helping a couple of hours each day in the barn. Now, I'm not complaining, just telling the facts.

The long winter evenings we used to have together are no more. By the time the chores are done, supper eaten, dishes washed, and everybody showered, it is time to get the children to bed. Hubby is conked out on the recliner from working so hard all day. So guess who gets to settle arguments, put on diapers and pajamas, tell bedtime stories, tuck the little ones to bed, and rock the baby? Good old Mom, who by this time is exhausted too.

This hectic lifestyle is not what I would choose, but I want to accept it and make the best of it. Those times when I'm physically and emotionally low, the Lord carries me. Maybe someday things will be different. Please sign me,

—*Overwhelmed on the Farm*, March 2002

Not Everyone Can Be a Farmer

I am writing this article because we rarely see our side of the story presented. Are we such a rare family? Does no one else experience life as we do? By now you are wondering what I am talking about.

Well, first of all, we don't live on a farm. Secondly, we are a happy family. I know a farm is a wonderful place to live, for I grew up on a farm and had a very happy childhood. My husband, however, never lived on a farm, but he had a happy childhood too.

My husband's dream did not include farming—he works away from home five days a week. When we married, actually before marriage, his dream became mine.

I realized that some things were going to be different, with Daddy gone all day. One is that Mama has the care and discipline of the children to herself while Daddy is at work. This can be overwhelming, especially if we don't discipline consistently or spend enough time with our little ones.

This burden on the mother can be greatly lightened if the children get to talk with Daddy before he leaves in the morning, and if they know there will be follow-up discipline if needed when he gets home.

It is often pointed out that a day laborer is gone from dawn till dusk and has no time for his family. But this should not be. We feel so fortunate to be able to work alongside Daddy every evening. In the summer, it is yard and garden work, and in the winter it is shopwork. If Daddy has to go away after work, the children usually get to go along. We feel that is such a privilege, especially when we hear how some farmers' wives must put the children to bed themselves because the husband is out late in the field or barn.

I don't want this to sound as if I am holding up one occupation above another. Rather, I am asking a simple question. Does a simple Christian lifestyle depend so much on our occupation? We feel it is possible to get into the rut of spending too much time away from the family, no matter what we do for a living. In other words, farming in itself is not the answer to all our problems. Neither is some other job in a suitable environment.

But if there is a sincere desire, we should be able to find time for our families and for those better things in life. That is what will count in eternity.

—A young wife, with the encouragement of her husband,
January 2002

We know that not everyone is cut out to be a farmer, and there are other suitable occupations as well. In the words of one of our farm writers . . . "I do not necessarily promote farming as the sole Christian way. I recall that Joseph was a carpenter, Peter was a fisherman, Paul was a tentmaker, Luke was a physician, Matthew was a tax collector, and Simon was a tanner."

—J. S., February 1994

Farmer at Heart

He measures, chalks, and saws. He nails it into place.
He carries boards and sheeting, a tool belt at his waist.

Though his work he does enjoy, his thoughts still often roam
To hopes he has of farming his own small fields at home.
So dreams are laid aside till debts are in control;
He's gone to work in carpentry, but farming's still his goal.
He goes to work without complaint, but while he works he
    dreams
Of harnesses a'jangling while working his own team.
Of plowing furrows 'midst the scent of fresh-turned sod,
Listening to the songs of birds, his heart attuned to God.
Spurred on by dreams of someday managing the land—
He is at heart a farmer with a hammer in his hand.

—By his wife, April 2018

The Risk in Amish Business

Because of the ever-rising price of land, many Amish are no longer exclusively farming. Some have shops or stores on their farms; others have shops or stores, period. There are dry goods, hardware, furniture, and bookstores; harness, buggy, bicycle, motor, axle, and machine shops. There are many woodworking shops in various states making anything from kitchen cabinets to trim and molding in all shapes and styles. The list could go on and on.

What effect is this switch from farming to shops and stores having on our way of life? For example, while visiting an Amish business I saw the owner's eleven-year-old daughter running a photocopier. Isn't that quite a contrast to other girls her age who are gathering eggs from the henhouse? Are we aware of the influences and taking precautions?

Five years ago, a university professor in upstate New York studied the rise of Amish businesses and published an article with the title "The Opening of Amish Society: Cottage Industry as Trojan Horse." Are shops and stores a "Trojan horse" for our Amish way of life?

—D. L., February 1997

A Connection with the Land

The following two selections are part of longer articles and are, for me, two of the most beautiful pieces of prose I found reading over fifty years of *Family Life*. Reading the connections these two men had to the earth, I had to wonder what a modern farmer on a big tractor might have written.

Once Upon a Stomach

From my earliest years, I have loved nature. As a young man, I found no peers who shared that love. So I squelched it, kept it a rather private thing, was a little ashamed of it. I didn't enjoy manly things such as Honda engines and high-paying carpenter jobs.

A stigma hangs over the person who stops his work to listen to a meadowlark. And to actually lie on your back and look at the sky in this modern world is a sign of financial irresponsibility.

Finally today, for the first time this summer, I did something about it. In the middle of a sunny forenoon, I sank to the ground in the middle of my grass field and did "nothing" for fifteen minutes—out of sight lying on my stomach, observing the "grassroots jungle." It was glorious.

If you've never observed what color sunshine is, lie on your stomach in a grass field. Sunshine makes the multitude of grass stems many different hues of green; the more direct the sunshine, the yellower the hue.

Down there in the wet shade, a small brown slug slid, eyestalks moving constantly. A red ant moved along up into the jungle, climbing fluidly from one stem to another. An inchworm found my hand. He was still young and his inches small. He measured my index finger at twenty-seven inches. A hover fly appeared silently and sat on a grassy stem . . . then sat on my notebook . . . and then on my pen. Quite a handsome fellow, his wings glinted with rainbow colors.

The wind swished through the wild cherry trees in the fencerow and made my jungle surroundings sway. But down in my grass hollow, I felt almost nothing. Over in the fencerow a song sparrow lifted his voice in a simple hymn. A tree swallow chattered as he sailed by. Mr. Mockingbird rattled off his row of thrice-repeated phrases.

I rolled onto my back and looked into the eye of infinity. I closed my eyes and focused on the sense of touch: fingers of sun warmth on my face. How absolutely marvelous and relaxing . . .

And then, the jingle of harness! I leapt to my feet. Was that Neighbor Daniel coming to mow my grass field? Catching me lying on my back on a sunny midmorning with work waiting? I headed in, pretending to be a good, solid, run-of-the-mill materialist, but feeling more refreshed than I had all summer. And don't you dare tell anyone!

—J. K. S., March 2020

A Plowman's Joy

Together the two red-tailed hawks circle in the blue sky, the wind rushing through their pinions. They dip and dive and ride the air thermals rising off the fields. In graceful flight, they follow the contour of the Conestoga Valley and look down on the farmland spread out below.

They can see the Amish and Mennonite farmers with their teams of horses and mules, and their tractors, turning the soil in long ribbons, while big fluttering clouds of gulls on long stiff wings wait to settle behind the plows and feast on earthworms.

Among the plowmen am I. I flip the reins and draw my eyes away from the sky. The three horses hitched to the triple tree strain in their harnesses with a willingness that comes after a long winter break. The wobbly lead wheel adds its own squeaky notes to the singing of the birds and the squawking of the gulls. A single brown ribbon of earth unfurls from my plow.

My thoughts go to the red-tailed hawks unleashing their spirited energy in the sky. Winter is only a memory, and I can see joy in their flight. Though I am grounded, I feel like I'm flying with the hawks.

I rest the horses at the end of the field by the tree row and watch their sides heave in steady rhythm. The smell of their sweat mixes with the smell of newly turned earth. The ground under the hackberries and old crabapple tree is carpeted in blue from the blooming grape hyacinth. From somewhere nearby a song sparrow sings and a robin carries building material for a nest up into one of the trees.

I could have used the sulky plow and ridden on a seat, but I enjoy walking and the sense of being connected with something that has changed little, and dates back centuries, all the way to olden times. As my bare feet follow the damp new furrow, I am practically following in the footsteps of ancient man.

I click to the horses, and their muscles ripple and stretch taut, and another strip of soil is turned. The uncaring blade cuts through the yellow wood sorrel and dandelions, the green rosettes of watercress and plantains. A field mouse's nest is upturned, and its squirming occupants suddenly find themselves exposed to a watchful dog.

A long irregular line of geese flies overhead, heading north just as they did in the days when the early settlers walked behind their teams of horses or oxen. The seasons still change. Like the greening of the woodland, this is the beginning of a new crop. The farmer plants, then waits for harvesttime while God sends down his blessing in life-giving rain and sunshine.

Swiftly the season advances. Now I am riding on the disc behind five horses. While we rest under the apple trees, a gust of wind sends the white petals snowing down around us. I watch, fascinated, as Whitey, the middle horse, swivels his ears back and forth while the petals fall around his head and cling to his mane.

The killdeers are calling noisily out in the field. They probably have an unlined nest with four eggs in it somewhere on top of the plowed furrows. I have never been as good as Dad in finding a nest and sparing it. Skillfully, he would guide the horses' plunging hooves around the nest, and the disc would just miss it by inches.

The years moved swiftly by, too, and memory sweetens with time. Already many years ago, I left my parents' farm in the fertile Piedmont region of Pennsylvania. I am thankful to have grown up on a farm. It was these small fragments that gave this young plowman much joy. In looking back, I consider the experience to have been a gift from my parents, a gift from the plow, and above all, a gift from God.

—Russell L. Stauffer, April 2011

* * *

Plowing Song

>Come, Sam! And Charlie, Perry, Mike!
>Now, Prince, you're slower than I like.
>We've half a field or more to go—
>I'd think you horses ought to know
>We need to plow while it is fit.
>If you would hurry just a bit;
>I know you're tired, and so am I,
>We'll rest tonight, then, by and by.
>You've loafed around all winter now—
>Come, boys, come on, I want to plow!
>>—By Joyce, for Daddy, May 2015

SEVEN

Church

IN THE AMISH WORLD, the church "congregation" can be quite different from English (non-Amish) churches. The reasons for this should be clear by now. Much mention is made of the concept of *Gelassenheit* (described in the first excerpt below). Rites of passage, such as baptism, marriage, and death, have their own traditions, many of which have changed very little, from ordination of new ministers to footwashing at communion. Yet church *Ordnung* (or rules) vary much more than we might expect from one congregation to the next. The Pennsylvania German language further reinforces the "otherness" and separation from the outside world, of being in the world but not of it. Many books have been written on all of this, but I found that these selections provide an inside look at that which most of us on the outside never see or experience. Being Amish isn't just a "Sunday thing." In many ways, worship services are the ultimate expression of being Amish, the "well" to which they go for refreshment, but also sometimes the source of controversy and even agonizing division. Here then in simple language are the basics of the Amish congregation.

Gelassenheit—*a Bible Principle*

The meaning of the German word *Gelassenheit* is "yielding, res-ignation, and inner surrender of one's self-will." Our forefathers stressed this term in their writings. *Gelassenheit* is the first step to true Christian brotherhood. It is the overcoming of selfish-ness. The conquering of everything personal and self-centered in the expression of brotherly love. It is also the renunciation of force.

For a church to function properly, there needs to be a com-pliance to its standards and practices. Disobedience is a sign of rebellion to God. *Gelassenheit* conveys this understanding of obedience.

Order in the church

The church is set up to deal with this problem of self-will. One of them is the *Ordnung*, or set of standards. The *Ordnung* is to define and restrain all self-assertive and manipulative be-havior. Another function is to decide what position to take that will not destroy its value system. For instance, the church has to control technology, and technology dare not control the church.

One of the major objectives of *Gelassenheit* is the rejection of pride, and an emphasis on humility. In no way, whether in dress, conduct, or attitudes may a person raise himself above his fellow brethren. A Christian must give up all desire to be distinct. He must give up his every wish to advance in personal power, wealth, or status.

The idea is that our time and our possessions are not our own. We are but stewards, and must give account to God for them. This does two things. It keeps us from spending our profit for personal luxuries, and it puts us under obligation to share our goods with those in need.

Nonresistance and non-swearing of oaths

Here the spirit of *Gelassenheit* is again evident. By refusing to take an oath, we are freed from taking part in the military system, the police force, or judicial obligations. We believe there is a place for these powers, but not within the church.

Plain dress

Most people in the world wear clothes to enhance their appearance, show off their bodies, or demonstrate their wealth. This is an expression of self-will, and is an attempt to raise oneself above our fellows.

Every individual could decide his own standards of plainness, and some church groups do that. But we insist on a uniformity of dress decided by church consensus. There are two reasons for this. Because self-will must yield to conform to church standards, and second, it removes the lure of competition. If we all dress alike, we are all on the same level. A uniform plain dress also provides an escape from the fashions of this world.

A Plain lifestyle

Our home furnishings and our way of living ought to be plain and simple so as not to appear more wealthy than others. Because we do not feel that evil resides in certain things themselves, but in their effect on our lives, the church decides to tolerate those things that are conducive to *Gelassenheit*, and to avoid those things that destroy Christian values. For example, we feel the ownership of automobiles destroys *Gelassenheit*, yet we can make a controlled use of them by hiring them. Motor vehicles have been a prominent factor in destroying home life.

Church leadership

When it comes to selecting leaders in the church, there are also checks and balances that function in a spirit of *Gelassenheit*.

By using the lot, no one can manipulate things according to his own thinking. The final decision rests with God. What is important is that a minister be yielded to God. Humility is the quality most appreciated in a leader.

A plural ministry prevents too much authority in one person. The decisions of the ministry are subject to approval by the laity, and it needs to be a unanimous decision.

Gelassenheit in baptism

It is a sign of repentance and of submission to God in all areas of life—a covenant to live by the power of powerlessness. It is renouncing all pride and self-will.

Gelassenheit in communion

The preparation for communion starts at the *Ordnung* services. This is a time of examining ourselves for whether our vows at baptism are still being kept. Communion is to show our love and harmony in the church, and not the other way around.

At communion there is emphasis on the love of Christ in bringing salvation, and on our obedience to his will. Our oneness together is also stressed; we are no more individuals.

The footwashing ceremony signifies a servant attitude, and the love that dwells among the brethren and sisters. Almsgiving is likewise an expression of *Gelassenheit*, as we share of our goods with the needy.

Discipline in the church

If someone is disobedient or falls into sin, *Gelassenheit* is there to help him be restored again. The church cannot tolerate disobedience. Discipline, however, is not intended as an outward use of force to make someone submit. Rather, it is to bring about an inward repentance and a renewed surrendering to

God. Therefore, discipline is the highest form of love within the brotherhood.

Discipline does three things. (1) It helps the sinner to repent. (2) It protects the church from sin. (3) It protects the reputation of the church to the outside world.

All these matters help us renounce self and our self-will, and enable us to function within the brotherhood in a spirit of love. All these principles grow out of the life, teachings, and death of Christ, our perfect example of *Gelassenheit*.

—Deacon Paul A. Kline, March 2017

The Household of Faith

A young man was visiting in the home of his uncle. During their conversation, the visitor remarked, "I see no need to be part of a brotherhood. I can serve God in my own way."

They were seated in front of a fireplace, watching the glowing embers. Silently the uncle arose, and with a small shovel he removed a red coal and placed it away from the fire. For a few minutes, the ember continued to glow, but then it slowly died out.

"There is a lesson here," the uncle pointed out. "That coal would still be burning if I had not taken it away from the fire. Alone, it soon cooled and lost its glow. It is the same with us humans. None of us can stand alone. We need the support of the brotherhood to walk the way of truth and remain steadfast in the faith."

All the members have their part to contribute to the church. This includes the laity as well as the ministry. Every church brotherhood which seeks to maintain a clear vision of purity and separation from the world will need guidelines and standards. This should not be left to the individual to make his own application of Scripture.

There is also the danger that a church group may sink into a dead formalism and legalism, following a set pattern, but without love or conviction. Love is the greatest essential in the spiritual vitality of the church. Love is a life of giving.

—David Bender, May 2012

* * *

Sunday Scramble

Oh, Mama, hurry, it is late!
And nearly time to go!
The dinner's in the oven now,
Anne, must we move so slow?
I need the comb that Sammy has;
I cannot find my socks!
My Sunday hat got sat on, flat!
My bonnet, Mom, is lost.
Run, turn the stove down, Susie,
And don't forget the purse.
We hurried the whole mile to church,
And lo! We were the first!

—S. and E. W., August/September 2014

The Games Our Children Play

I still remember that warm summer day when we children assembled in a circle in our front yard to "play church." I happened to be the "preacher" that day, and when I stood up to tell my listeners about God's greatness and how Jesus came to the world so we could all go to heaven, I put great emphasis on some of the words, just as I had heard real ministers do. Suddenly a smirk replaced the earnest look on someone's face, and before we knew it, we were all giggling.

Immediately, Mother was at our side. "You may play church," she explained, hushing our laughter quickly with the sadness in her voice. "But you must never, never make fun of church, not even in play. Church is sacred, and not something to laugh about."

I suppose that was one of the first times in my young life that I realized the seriousness of certain things in life—not just when we were working but also when we were playing.

I often wonder what motivates our little children to organize their small benches, get out their songbooks, and then with their dolls in their arms, settle down to "play church." How earnestly they open their throats to the old slow tunes sung by their parents and grandparents in church. Then one of them gets up to tell the story of Jonah, who was swallowed by a whale, or Daniel, who was thrown into a den of lions.

When they kneel for silent prayer, a figure in the background pauses in her work to bow her own head in reverence until the prayer is over. She remembers a certain day in her childhood when she, too, "played church" in the shade of a weeping willow tree. She prays that God will guide and direct her little ones to the real faith they were now imitating.

—Anonymous, August/September 1994

* * *

Ordinations in the Church

The first ordination service I can recall and the one I probably remember the best took place when I was ten years old. Ordinations are conducted at the close of communion services. The reason I remember it so well is because my oldest sister's husband was chosen and ordained that day as a minister of the Word. Nine years later he was ordained as a bishop, in which capacity he served an additional fifty years. Altogether, he labored in the ministry of the church for more than sixty years.

Amish ministers are chosen by lot, patterned after the example given in the first chapter of Acts. That portion of Scripture is always read before an ordination. I do not know of anyone who believes that the lot was always used in the early Christian church. Yet that is the way ministers have been selected ever since the Amish came to America.

Before the lot is cast, the church has its duty to do—to come before God in prayer and fasting, and then to nominate brethren who appear to be qualified for the ministry. In many communities, three votes are required to put someone into the lot, although in some areas only two votes are needed. The hope and prayer of the church is that God will then choose the right one.

Not for self-exaltation

When a minister is selected in our Amish churches, a person's own opinion of himself is given no consideration. One of the scriptural references that support this is found in 2 Corinthians 10:18, "For not he that commendeth himself is approved, but whom the Lord commendeth."

In our churches the male applicants for baptism are asked whether they would be willing to accept the call to the ministry if it should come. They must answer in the affirmative before they receive baptism.

In our Plain churches the bishops receive no wages and must spend a lot of time and effort in their work for the church. This is a heavy load to carry, and is accepted only because God and the church request it—and not by personal choice.

Ordination practices

We adults know that ministers are only human and are subject to mistakes the same as anyone else. In fact, their very position of leadership puts them in a vulnerable place, and the temptation may come to misuse their power and authority in an attempt to get their own way.

The question might be asked, "Does selecting the ministry by the use of the lot always work out satisfactorily for the good of the church?" Of course not. Anything in which humans have a part is subject to failure, but this is not necessarily the fault of the system. Rather, it is the fault of human imperfection and error.

—David Wagler, October 1996

Called to Serve

My hands felt clammy in my lap. With each exhaling breath an inaudible prayer arose from deep within my bosom, "Thy will be done." The very air seemed charged with expectancy in this solemn and sacred moment.

Ordinations are a necessary part in the growth and continuation of the church. On this day this became increasingly real as I heard my husband's name being read off from the list in the bishop's hand. The time had come for the revealing of a new minister to fill the vacancy in our district.

There were six men with bowed heads sitting on the front bench. Each one held a black *Ausbund* in his hands. My husband sat first. A wave of emotions washed over me as I watched the bishop reach for my husband's book and leaf through it. He did not hand it back. Those who have experienced the same will be able to identify with the feelings that surged through my being as the reality soaked in. A new calling rested on our shoulders.

To ministers' wives, it cannot be overemphasized what our moral support may mean to our husbands. They did not choose this position. It will mean sacrificing time and study when outdoor work beckons on a beautiful spring day. Our hand on his shoulder as he sits in meditation will speak volumes to his heart. Children can be taught to do more than their usual share of chores so Dad can have his study time.

Let us not cease to uplift the ministers in our daily prayers. They are called to labor in God's vineyard. Our support will ease their burden.

—*A minister's wife*, May 2017

A Most Sacred Call

We went to the ordination,
To see how the lot would fall—
To fill the spot that was vacant,
Which man the Lord would call.
Soon we'd know the will of the Father,
Whom he'd chosen to fill this place—
A calling that must be the highest
E'er laid on the poor human race.

Then the words of the visiting preacher
Struck my heart like a two-edged sword,
For he asked, "What's the highest calling
Ever given to man by the Lord?"

He went on and said, "You mothers,
At home with your children so small—
Yours is a very great calling,
Yours is a most sacred call.
The ministry's load would be lighter
If parents would all strive to guide
The precious wee lambs to the Father,
And teach them in him to confide."

—*A mother*, March 2001

That the Sheep Might Be Fed

With a sigh, Alvin Yoder slipped to his knees. Tomorrow it was to be his turn to preach the main sermon. What did God want him to say?

It was Sunday morning and the deacon had finished reading the chapter. With a prayer in his heart, Alvin stood up to speak.

Ervin Miller sat with bowed head and uplifted heart. His wife lay ill in a hospital many miles away. Now the minister's words felt like a tonic on his anxious heart.

Hannah Bontrager was also drinking in the encouraging words. She was discovering that life as a schoolteacher could be very taxing. But now she would take one day at a time, trusting in God's help.

Alvin not only encouraged, he also warned. Young folks sat up soberly, challenged to face life more seriously and to seek God while he was still to be found.

But not everyone was favorably impressed with the sermon. In fact, some persons in the audience heard very little of it. Head-nodders disgraced the room. Ammon King felt guilty as he shook himself half awake. He had worked so hard the past week.

Kathy Beachy wasn't particularly sleepy, but she found it difficult to concentrate on a sermon with the boys sitting in full view before her. The excitement of fancying herself in love dulled her spiritual hunger.

Gerald Wengerd listened half-heartedly. The sermons lacked zest, the power of the Holy Spirit. He was glad that he and his wife would soon be changing churches.

There were others who also got little spiritual nourishment from the day's sermon. They didn't stop to realize they were the ones at fault, that it was their ill feelings that kept them from hearing the message God wanted them to hear.

Alvin Yoder had come to church that morning with a burden on his heart, and when he drove home that afternoon with his family, part of the burden was still there. Was there anything he could do about it?

—*One of the Sheep*, August/September 1993

* * *

Some Questions about Baptism

For our Anabaptist forefathers, baptism was a very serious issue, often a matter of life and death. Thousands of them died as martyrs because of their Christian faith, and because they were willing to be baptized upon that faith.

No other issue caused as much controversy during the sixteenth-century as whether or not infants should be baptized. Today, infant baptism may not be of such concern to us, yet it is very important to have a scriptural understanding of the innocence of children, and to realize why they should not be baptized.

Why do children not need baptism?

"Christ accepted the children, and through grace and mercy promised them the kingdom of heaven, but not on account of or by baptism. For He neither baptized them nor commanded them to be baptized, but laid His hands upon them and blessed them" (Dietrich Philip, *Enchiridion*, p. 43).

Because of its deep significance, baptism must only be administered to those persons who have been made worthy of it by the blood of Christ. Unless there is evidence of repentance and faith, and unless there is sincerity and a desire to truly serve God, the applicant is not ready for baptism. The church has a responsibility to prove the candidates for baptism.

Is their conversion genuine?

In our time of freedom and prosperity, there are artificial pressures and influences that lead people to "join the church" without being scripturally qualified to belong . . .

"All my friends my age are in the instruction class, and I don't want to be left out."

"My parents are urging me to join the church."

"I've had a good time, but maybe I ought to settle down now. One never knows about tomorrow."

"My girlfriend and I want to get married. So that means we need to be baptized first. The church won't marry us unless we're members."

Some of the above reasons for baptism are not wrong in themselves. But there must be deeper and more meaningful reasons than these before a person is ready for baptism.

God would have his children to be in earnest about the Christian life. Perhaps the greatest threat to the church today is to baptize those who are half-hearted and lukewarm, or who come to the church for carnal and selfish motives.

Of what is outward baptism a testimony?

The martyrs of the sixteenth century placed great emphasis on the role of the church. Their vision of a biblical church was a disciplined body of believers who rebuked sin and led holy lives, and who had been baptized upon their common faith and commitment to God.

Within this Christian brotherhood, each member's personal identity and individualism fades into the background and is lost in the larger witness of the church. Thus it is Christ's church rather than the individual that becomes a light to the world and the salt of the earth.

Water baptism is a sign and testimony of the dying of the old man and the resurrection of the new. But it is more. Baptism is also a pledge and a covenant before God and man, which is the church of God.

—Anonymous, July 1993

* * *

Hands at Communion

Hands—
Reaching for communion's bread.
Gnarled, work-roughened, calloused hands
Cupping the communion bread
One last time.
Young, smooth, pink-nailed hands
Touching the communion bread
For the first time.
Hands in the midst of midlife strains,
Nails chipped, fingers cracked with darker stains.
Graceful hands, holding lightly,
Twisted hands, holding tightly.
Many hands, from all stages of life,
Accepting communion's bread
As one.

Scores of hands—
Reaching, cupping, grasping, holding,
Outstretched for holy nourishment from the loaf,
Yielding unto fellowship,
Summoned to the common goal
In preparation for the paths ahead.
Hands which caressed the softness
Of the white communion bread,
Now folded into acquiescence.
Ready to work again

At tomorrow's labors,
With strength gained of communion's bread
Today.

—Darla Weaver, December 2020

A Special Loaf

When you partake of the bread at communion, have you ever considered what the loaf consists of? When my husband was ordained deacon, it became my duty, as his wife, to bake the communion loaf. As I was mixing the dough, I was somewhat awed that the bread I was making was supposed to be a symbol of Jesus' body. It was hard for me to stir it together like common, everyday bread. Somehow it should be more specially done, it seemed to me.

I thought of all the members who would partake of the bread on the coming Sunday. As I kneaded the dough, I thought of each member in turn, and breathed a prayer for each one. Although I didn't know what each person struggles with, for some of them I did. Some have an illness, some are elderly. Others have struggles with disobedient children. Younger families are coping with a heavy workload. And what about the young man whose girlfriend decided to end their friendship? The list went on and on.

By the time I was finished remembering everyone in prayer, the loaf was nicely kneaded. To me, it was no longer "just a loaf." It was Jesus' loaf, and I am thankful that I could consider myself as . . .

—*One of the pieces*, October 2015

* * *

Footwashing: Symbol of Humility

Of all the ordinances of Christ, footwashing is probably the most unpopular and disregarded. There is something deeply humbling about the practice. Kneeling down before another is in itself an insult to pride; to actually wash his feet is even more so. But its unpopularity makes it no less important and necessary. The most crucial point is that it brings us all down to the same level, rich and poor, noble or slaves.

Most [non-Amish] churches have rejected footwashing. Others leave it optional. Although it would seem to us that Jesus was very clear in his teaching on footwashing, this has not kept men from trying to explain it away.

Jesus clearly stated the reason in John 13:14–17. He, as Master and Lord, humbled himself to wash the disciples' feet. Since the servant is not greater than his Lord, it is a small thing in comparison for us to wash each other's feet. If we object to bowing down and washing the feet of our brethren, we are in effect considering ourselves greater than our Lord.

In article 11 of our confession of faith, footwashing is stated to have still another significance. It is a sign of the true washing— the washing and purification of the soul in the blood of Christ.
—Isaac R. Horst, April 1995

True Love in Action

Our twice-yearly communion service is always a special occasion for me. After I was baptized and joined the congregation as a teenager, I was then allowed to participate as a member. Today I saw true love being lived. Not a romantic relationship, not a marriage relationship, nor even love within a family. The love I saw today surpassed by far any of the above. I saw the love of Christ in action.

The service was conducted by Bishop Titus, Preachers Enos and Leroy, and Deacon Matthew. Enos had the first part concerning the creation of the world until the time of the flood. Then Leroy spoke of the patriarchs, stopping as soon as he had the children of Israel safely in the Promised Land.

Bishop Titus then reviewed the Old Testament prophecies of the coming of the Messiah, moving quickly on to the suffering and death of Christ. Near the end of his sermon, Titus told of the Last Supper.

At that time Matthew and Leroy brought in the bread and wine. With ritualistic care, they placed it on the table. The entire congregation was summoned to stand in prayer, and a blessing was asked on the bread. The bishop took a morsel of the bread for himself, and then handed a morsel to every member in turn, beginning with the men and moving over to the women's side. The wine was treated in the same way, with everyone drinking a small sip from the common cup.

All this was impressive, but the touching part of love in action was yet to come. Basins of water were brought in and set around the room, along with towels. Then all the members prepared for the ceremony of footwashing, as taught by Christ to his disciples on the night when he was betrayed. Men with men, and women with women, the members paired off and moved to the nearest basin. One person would sit down and the other would take the towel and wrap it around the waist, kneel down, and wash the other's feet. They then exchanged places so that everyone had a turn to both wash and be washed. On finishing, they gave each other a kiss of peace. On this solemn and joyful occasion, social and class differences disappear. The wealthy and the pauper, the respected and the lowly, all are given the same status and the same recognition.

I saw my grandfather assisting the aged and handicapped Jonathan with footwashing. Jonathan is bent with arthritis, but determined to take part, not only to be washed but to wash another's feet. He needs a helping hand even to walk, so this is no small endeavor.

The friendship between these two old men is in itself a thing of rare beauty, not the least because my grandfather is so hard of hearing as to be legally deaf, while Jonathan is too weak to speak loudly enough for Grandpa to hear him.

Grandpa helped him make his way to the nearest basin. Carefully he guided Jonathan to the seat; tenderly he washed his feet for him. The left foot is semi-paralyzed from a stroke, and Grandpa had to lift it in and out of the basin.

Then came the hard part, the part that was most touching. Jonathan was determined that he would wash his partner's feet, too, in order to feel he had truly fulfilled his Master's command.

Anxiously steadying Jonathan, Grandpa sat down on the bench and put his own feet into the tub, one at a time. Jonathan bends over with difficulty, so Grandpa had to lift each foot up high so Jonathan could dry them. All the time my grandfather had a firm hold on Jonathan's arm to prevent him from falling. To give the kiss of peace, Grandpa needed to bend way down to accommodate Jonathan's bent back. Then with the help of three other men nearby, Jonathan moved back to his bench. Grandpa helped him put on his socks and shoes before he took care of his own.

How easy it would have been to tell Jonathan he did not need to wash someone else's feet. How easy it would have been to dismiss the very real person inside that twisted body. What I saw today, what these men did for Jonathan, was indeed true love in action. It was the spirit of Christ living in the hearts of men.

—J. M. Z., October 2012

* * *

Bearing One Another's Burdens

It is a dramatic, frightening experience when a big barn burns. The barn may have stood there for generations, season after fruitful season. Each summer the loft has been filled with hay and straw, and each winter the mows are emptied again.

Blizzards and summer storms alike have bombarded the sturdy walls, but the barn has stood firm.

Then, picture, if you can, dark thunderclouds passing over in the night and a jagged flash of lightning zigzagging down from the sky and striking the stately old barn. The sleeping farmer and his family are rudely awakened. The fire is rapidly turning into an inferno. It seems like ages until the fire trucks arrive.

The next few hours are a nightmare. Neighbors huddle in a semicircle, their somber faces illuminated by the flashing red lights of the fire engine against the orange backdrop of the flames. Steam hisses as thousands of gallons of water arc through the air and fall upon the fire. There is a muffled crash as the roof caves in.

Every farmer fears a major fire. He knows that what has happened to others can also happen to him. That in itself is a good reason to willingly help rebuild and to share the burden.

In our Amish and Old Order Mennonite communities, thankfully, a fire is only part one of a continued story. The disaster becomes an opportunity, a challenge, a rallying of the entire community to rebuild. In a true act of compassion the neighbors flock to the scene and help clean up the mess. Plans are laid for a new barn. Hope replaces despair. Trees are felled and sawed into lumber, the foundation poured, building supplies assembled.

The climax is the day of the barn raising. People come by the hundreds, and they come with a mind to work. The barn raising is also a social event, but that is merely a bonus—the real reason is to give tangible expression to the golden rule, and to bear one another's burdens as the New Testament teaches.

Somehow barn raisings have come to be a very popular news event. Self-invited reporters are eager with their questions and their cameras. Can we blame them? After all, the news is flooded with horror stories and corruption, with wars and violence. To present the positive side is a welcome change—a refreshing story of unselfish attitudes and a warm group spirit. Can you imagine a more uplifting topic than the photo of several hundred men swarming over the framework of a new barn? This symbolizes old-fashioned values. It is a reminder of a time when it was not uncommon to care about one's neighbors.

Of course, it makes us uncomfortable to be so much in the public eye, and I'm sure the flattery is not good for us at all. It would be nice if we could avoid that. But I trust the unwelcome publicity will not deter us from going on and helping each other as before. Nor do we wish to selfishly limit our help to our own people—we should be ready to assist others, too, even those who seem to resent us.

—J. S., November 1995

The Church's Glory

A man once called on a clergyman, so the story goes, with the purpose of finding a suitable church that he and his family might attend.

"Now before we get started," he informed the preacher, "I mean to tell you that I'm far too busy to become involved with church activities. All I'm looking for is a place to bring my wife and children to hear some preaching."

"It appears to me," the minister returned, "that you are at the wrong place. I've heard of such a church and, if you please, I can take you there."

So the minister showed him across town to an old, dilapidated building. "The folks that attended this church were much like you," the preacher explained, a tone of sadness in his voice. "They were too busy minding their own business. They had no time to devote to God and the church."

Do we honestly appreciate our church and brotherhood as God would have us do? Or have we become as self-centered and indifferent as the man in the above story?

When doling out the bread and wine of communion, the bishop may use the illustration of wheat ground into flour. Just as the kernels of wheat are so intermingled in the bread that they can no longer be separated, so should the body of believers be.

Likewise the wine. The grapes have been pressed and strained, losing all traces of individuality to become a substance of much greater value and service at the Lord's communion table.

Life is no longer about me and mine. Instead, we have blended together in unity with a common vision, focused on serving Jesus and meeting the needs of those around us, all that being about our Father's business consists of (see Luke 2:49).

Unity and peace within the church has become especially difficult in this permissive society. Sports, vacations, and an easy lifestyle are idolized. Labor-saving devices, electronics, and a host of other inventions constantly bombard and entice an already progressive generation. Remember, peace leads to prosperity, prosperity leads to pride, and pride leads to haughtiness and strife.

The church has withstood much hardship and conflict from within and from without. So far the church, albeit battered, has prevailed. But is it resilient enough to withstand what is quite possibly its last and greatest test—this silent, yet deadly struggle to remain humble pilgrims and strangers, pure and unspotted from the world, in the face of prolonged luxury, prosperity, and extravagance?

—*A deacon*, May 2014

A Handy Prayer List

A grandmother had been telling a Bible story to her grandchildren. Then she held up her left hand so all the children could see. "Look at my thumb and fingers," she said. "They remind me of the things I should pray for every day. My thumb is nearest to me, so I start by praying for my family, the ones who are dearest and nearest to me. I pray for my friends and neighbors, too. And I thank the Lord that he has blessed me with so many dear ones."

Grandma paused, but she was still holding her hand in the air. "Next to my thumb is my index finger," she said. "Years ago, my teacher used to point that finger at me in school. Sometimes our preachers shake this finger in church when they are warning us about dangers. So when I think of that finger, I pray for the teachers and preachers and the parents who have a great responsibility to guide those in their care."

The grandchildren were listening with interest. "My middle finger is the longest one," Grandma continued. "It stands above the others. This reminds me to pray for the rulers of our country and for all those in authority.

"The next finger is the weakest one. It makes me think of the poor and the sick and the helpless. I ask the Lord to supply their needs and to strengthen them in body and soul. And I also pray that if there is any way I can be a help to these people, I want to do my part."

With that, the grandmother came at last to her little finger. "This one stands for me," she said. "So I finish my prayer by praying for myself and all the things I need."

I have adapted the above little story from one I read in a church paper. It is a good lesson for all of us. Prayer is very much a part of every sincere Christian's life. A good look at the thumb and four fingers of each hand can be a "handy" prayer list.

—Anonymous, December 2012

* * *

Confessions of a Seeker

It has been almost twenty-three years that I came to the Amish church. The journey has been hard and rocky at times. It has also been rewarding. It is not easy to come from a worldly setting into the church. It is also not easy for the church to welcome those of us who grew up in the world.

We who want to join are often referred to as "seekers." In some ways, I do not like that term. We are all seeking the kingdom of God. However, I am still a seeker. Both seekers and those who grew up in the church need to have the same goal. We are all children of the same God, and our goal is to obey God's commandments and to love each other.

It has been somewhat of a lonely life. The church is made up of families, and my family is not part of this church. The church tries to be my family, but I have a different past than they do. A seeker needs the whole church, but also one specific family that he can feel a part of. I had that family until they moved to a new community. I miss being part of that family. I used to be able to go talk or just be with them.

My past is different from those who grew up in the church. Even though in many ways my past is not how I wish it was, I have to accept that. We need to remind ourselves that seekers cannot help how they were raised. They are looking for something better than they have, and it is up to us in the church to help them find it. We all need to be here to help each other.

The seeker needs to feel needed, but also should take time before becoming a member of the church. I was here for two and a half years before I became a member.

The seeker needs to be told the church's *Ordnung* from the very first. I did not know what to ask about when I first came. Most seekers are looking for a Plain church. It has been hard for me to understand why the Amish keep wanting more material things.

Likely every Plain person has an ancestor who joined the church from the "world." Every person who is a descendant of a seeker is benefiting from a church that welcomed that seeker.

—Lee W. Thiel II, October 2019

Living by Example

I grew up in a non-Amish family in Lancaster County. I watched as you lived your lives as Christians. I walked from covered bridge to covered bridge each day to observe your family life. When I hiked to a nearby farm to get some leather fixed, you spoke to me as if I mattered. At the Lancaster farmers' market, you talked to me with a twinkle in your eye concerning the best tomatoes and produce.

As I grew up, I found your guidebook, the Bible, and I sought to likewise live your faithfulness and devotion. This has brought me peace and joy. I learned how to forgive by observing your example. I doubt that I am the only one who has been affected by your lives. Thank you.

—*From a nearby state*, August/September 2020

EIGHT

Discipline

AS MENTIONED IN THE PRIOR CHAPTER, there are rules to be followed within the church. Some congregations are very conservative in their approach, others very liberal, but all must share certain basics in order to be considered Amish. However, specific rules, scriptural interpretations, and even individual personalities at times create conflict that may require discipline. Shunning, or the ban, the most severe form of discipline in the Amish church, is a concept that has often been misrepresented or misunderstood. One Amish man told me it is not always "applied correctly," since it should be practiced so as to bring the person back into the fold, not drive the person away. Forgiveness and repentance are part of the mix, or should be. Nevertheless, this form of excommunication does occur. When issues arise on a community level, a congregation may split. The Amish regret this, but they cannot always resolve differences when they arise. It is revealing to listen to the Amish speak about this topic—to get their perspective, and to leave ours behind for a while. Are you willing to listen before you judge?

The *Ordnung*

Clothing and Conduct in Swiss Laws

The German word *Ordnung* means "order" or "regulation." Twice each year before the semiannual communion service, Amish bishops state the congregation's rules at what is referred to as the *Ordnung Gemee*, or "council church." In a members' meeting after the preaching service, the bishop goes point by point through the *Ordnung* concerning attire and lifestyle. A wide variety of rules are covered, from the width of hat brims to the color of stoves, in order to maintain humility, simplicity, and uniformity in daily Christian living.

The Amish custom of stating the *Ordnung* to the members dates back many centuries to their Swiss fatherland. Before the Protestant Reformation, the Catholic Church had ecclesiastical courts that governed the morals and manners of the citizens. With the coming of the Reformation to some of the Swiss cantons, the responsibility of regulating citizens' lives was given to a secular tribunal chosen by the town council.

—David Luthy, July 1994

The Church's Duty to Discipline

A lot of negative things could be said about the Swiss attempt to control the lives of citizens. But let us keep in mind that a lot of negative things have been said about our Amish system of *Regel und Ordnungen*, too. For instance, the following points are often heard:

1. It is too legalistic, with too much emphasis on the letter.
2. It is like the Pharisees with their commandments of men.
3. It gives a false hope to people who comfort themselves that if they obey the *Ordnung*, that is all it takes.

All the above can be true. Indeed, they *will* be true if the *Ordnung* is abused or misused, or if the church is made up of carnal people.

Who is to decide what is proper and modest and practical? Shall this be left up to the individual? That is the popular spirit of our day—"My life is my own to live. No one has the right to tell me what to do or how to dress. My brother is not my keeper!"

But that is not the way of Christians who are serious about building up God's church to his honor and glory and want to keep it pure from all sin. It is not enough to merely encourage the brethren and sisters to dress simply, humbly, and modestly and then leave it to each one's discretion what that means. No, it is the church's duty as a brotherhood to interpret the Scriptures and to make practical applications of Bible principles as they pertain to everyday life. It is the church's duty, also, to use discipline in a scriptural way if members are not submissive.

—J. S., July 1994

More Than Suggestions

The world will never understand godly submission, nor will it practice it; yet curiously enough even in a permissive society there are laws, and the enforcement of those laws. There is submission to authority, although not always willingly. If there were no laws, no one would be safe on the streets, driving down the highway, or in the home. Without enforcement of the laws, all would be confusion. People obey, or they suffer the consequences. To be effective, a law must define what is permissible and what is not. It must also specify what the penalty will be if we violate that law.

This is really not so different from what God provides for us in his Word, but in a moral and spiritual sense. The Bible is specific in what is acceptable behavior for those who wish to live by its precepts. It also states the penalty for violating them. There are people who consider the commandments of the Bible to be good advice but not necessarily something to obey. No doubt they would like to change the Ten Commandments to "the Ten Suggestions."

—David Wagler, December 1998

The Right and Wrong Way to Disagree

The Bible places a high value on being of one heart and of one mind within the church. How is such unity achieved? One need not read very far in the old German hymns of the *Ausbund* to realize what a central role the church played in the lives of our martyr forefathers.

Of course, there will always be differences of opinion in any church. Not everyone will think exactly alike. We do not all have the same background of teaching and experience. Each of us is to a degree a product of his past.

Surely there is a scriptural way to express dissent within the church—a way that God can bless. There must be a right way to differ. Criticism can be constructive. A Christian can disagree without being disagreeable.

The wrong way

1. Not being supportive of the church.
2. Sowing discord among brethren.
3. Staying back from communion in protest.
4. Withdrawing into one's own shell.

The right way

1. A humble and respectful attitude.
2. A balanced interpretation of the Scriptures.

3. Presenting concerns directly to the ministry.

4. Exercise patience.

5. If action is necessary, let it be positive action.

Despite everything that we have advised to the contrary, there will be times when the individual needs to act against the counsel of the church to which he belongs. If error or drift persists and the church is not willing or able to make corrections, the day may come when it is advisable to look elsewhere— when one must become a doer and not just a critic.

It is desirable, and should be possible, to leave in a peaceful way without condemning one's former church. It becomes not so much a judgment of the church you leave as an honest attempt to find a better environment for yourself and your children.

One of the greatest risks is to disagree in such a way that we become separated from our brethren and become lone, unchurched Christians. Let us never be too sure of ourselves. When we disagree, may God preserve us from the pitfalls into which others have fallen. We are no better than they.

—Joseph Stoll, December 1995

Forgiveness

The Art of Peacemaking

Jacob and Levi had fallen out with each other on some small matter. They attended the same church, but now avoided each other. This worried Henry, the deacon, and he determined to heal the breach between the two men.

Henry stopped at Jake's house on his way to town. "What do you think of Levi by now?" he asked.

"I don't want to say too much, but I don't feel he's used me right. I get the impression he looks out only for himself."

"But," said the deacon, "you must admit he has a nice family, and he's very concerned to bring up his children in the fear of the Lord."

"Yes, I respect him for that. He is very concerned for his family."

The next day the deacon called at Levi's house and said, "Do you know what Jake says about you?"

Levi's smile turned into a scowl. "I don't know, but I can pretty well imagine what he says about me."

"Well, he says you are very concerned about your family, and he really respects you for that."

"You mean Jake said that about me?"

"Yes, I heard him say it. What's your opinion of Jake, if I may ask?"

Levi's scowl deepened. "I'd rather not say what I think of him."

"But you have to admit you won't find a more honest man."

"Yes, he is honest, but what has that to do with it?"

The next day Deacon Henry called on Jake again, and said, "Do you know what Levi was saying about you yesterday? He said you are very honest."

"You don't mean it!"

"I do. I heard it with my own ears."

The next Sunday after church, Jake and Levi were seen in friendly conversation.

We close by repeating the words of Jesus, "Blessed are the peacemakers: for they shall be called the children of God."

—Anonymous, December 2011

Nine Principles for Ending Broken Relationships

There are two basic things that can happen which cause broken relationships among Christians—(1) someone sins against you; (2) you sin against someone else. These sins may be great, or they may be quite trivial. The degree of transgression is not important. Anything that causes disharmony, however small, must be dealt with.

Some sins that cause discord are lying, not giving someone credit when it is due, not saying thank you, putting someone in a bad light in front of others, starting a rumor, resentment, envy, jealousy, talking about someone behind his back, and misjudging motives. Here are nine principles, based on Scripture, that will help us mend broken relationships:

Principle 1: Confess it to the Lord. This makes things right with God, which is the first step. But we can't stop there.

Principle 2: Make the first move. Don't wait for the other person to come to you. No matter who is in the wrong, if you are involved in a broken relationship, it is *your* problem. The thing that your brother or sister has against you may not even be something you have actually done. We must deny ourselves the pride that keeps us from mending broken relationships.

Principle 3: Do it quickly. The longer you think about the wrong between yourself and some other person, the bigger it becomes to you. We are a fellowship; we are all parts of one body. Thus when sin is marring a part of this body, it is our duty to mend it quickly before it spreads. That is why covering up a broken relationship with false on-the-surface "niceness" is so dangerous.

Principle 4: Meet the person face-to-face. Don't send someone else, or write a letter. By doing this, you can't see his face, you can't read the expression in his eyes, you can't shake his hand. It must be done in person. Jesus said, "*Go* to him . . ."

(Matthew 18:15–35). Of course, if you are separated by a thousand miles, you may have to settle for what is second best and write a letter.

Principle 5: Go in genuine love. If the mending isn't done in love, then it is false. That is even more deceptive than not going at all.

Principle 6: Go in the Spirit of peace and reconciliation. When you go to your brother, be sure you have already forgiven him in your heart for any wrong he may have done you. If you haven't forgiven him, don't go. Get on your knees first. Go to him with the single object of seeking peace. This isn't a contest to see who can have the last word or win an argument. Deny yourself the satisfaction of getting back at your brother.

Principle 7: Confess, apologize, and ask forgiveness. Don't justify yourself or make excuses for where you have failed. Don't be defensive. Apologize. Ask forgiveness. If it is the other way around and your brother has sinned against you, then your approach must be a little different. Tell your brother that you have forgiven him for what he has done. Even if he refuses to admit that he did wrong and doesn't apologize for his actions, you must still forgive him.

Principle 8: Let this end the matter. Leave the sinful action and talking about it all behind us. Don't let your mind dwell on it any further. Don't gossip about it. Forget it.

Principle 9: Forgive your brother again and again. Forgive a brother as often as he needs forgiveness. If we are not concerned about the broken relationships that separate us from our brethren, then how can we expect to have a good relationship with God?

—Monroe Beachy, November 2001

Shunning: The Ban

Questions and Answers on the Ban

1. What are the grounds for which a member should be expelled from the church?

The Bible teaches that three classes of people should not remain undisciplined within the church:

    a. He who is guilty of a "sin unto death" (1 Corinthians 6:9–10).

    b. He who refuses correction (Matthew 18:15–17).

    c. He who errs in doctrine (Titus 3:10).

2. What should be our feeling when a member needs to be excommunicated?

Great sadness that a member needs to be severed from the body of Christ. If we have the spirit of Christ, we will love the sinner as sincerely as we hate his sin.

3. What illustration did Jesus give that supports the concept of excommunication?

"If thy right eye offend thee, pluck it out, and cast it from thee," and "if thy right hand offend thee, cut it off, and cast it from thee" (Matthew 5:29–30).

4. What reason did Jesus give for taking such extreme measures?

Because it is better that one of the members should perish than the whole body be cast into hell (Matthew 5:29–30).

5. According to the Scriptures, what is excommunication designed to accomplish?

    a. That the church not become a partaker of sins and the leaven penetrate the whole lump. (See Galatians 5:9).

b. Secondly, that the sinner be brought to repentance—
   that he may be made ashamed and his be mortified
   thereby, but his spirit saved in the day of the Lord Jesus
   (1 Corinthians 5:5).

c. Thirdly, that the church of God not be evil spoken of or
   blasphemed on account of wicked members in it, and
   be answerable on their account before the Lord. (See
   Ezekiel 36:17–24.)

6. How is the ban and shunning most effective?
If it is undertaken in a scriptural manner—a sober and serious
call to repentance, "yet count him not as an enemy, but admon-
ish him as a brother" (2 Thessalonians 3:15). This means being
friendly and helpful, but not freely mingling with him socially
or in business. The ban should be a constant reminder to the
transgressor to repent.

7. What should be our feeling when the ban becomes necessary?
It should fill us with deep sorrow, nor should we cease from
praying for the expelled member's repentance. When he re-
pents, he should be welcomed back into the church with great
rejoicing.

*8. Is there not also a danger of being too strict and unyielding
with the ban?*
Yes, the ban, along with all other scriptural practices, has at
times been abused. This can happen when there are other motives besides love for the sinner and a zeal to keep the church
pure. These are abuses; they do not give us any excuse not to
make a scriptural application of the ban.

9. What changes have occurred in the past hundred years or so?
In recent years, there have been far too many regrettable
church divisions, both among the more conservative groups
and among those more progressive. In spite of this, or maybe

in part because of this, there are loopholes by which it is possible for a member of a nonconformed brotherhood to church-hop right on out into the world without ever being excommunicated.

10. What is the church's duty with regard to the ban?
Our responsibility as a church has not changed. The Scriptures give clear instructions. All discipline must be motivated by love, and applied in love and moderation. We need to uphold this doctrine, but not abuse it.

—Compiled from various sources, May 2020

No Need to Be Harsh

Over the years, I have discussed the subject of the ban with numerous persons from general society. Many of them stumble at the concept, yet in reality in our modern times they often practice a form of separation that is much harsher than God's, even though they consider themselves tolerant.

For instance, three brothers were the heirs when their mother died. One of them was the executor. The other two blamed him for claiming more than his share. Therefore, they are no longer on speaking terms.

Yet nowhere in the New Testament are we forbidden to speak with an excommunicated member. If we have a "don't speak to them" mentality, I fear the results will not be good. Our attitude shows through to a much greater extent than we often realize, indicating whether we have true love or not.

—*A Kentucky reader*, August/September 2020

Leaving the Faith

Crying and Praying

I was forced to decide where my duties lie, in keeping my first promise to my church or obeying the pleadings of my husband to go with him to a more liberal church. I have not regretted that I stayed, although doing so was and still is very hard, for it separated the family. If it weren't for the prayers from fellow pilgrims, I would not be able to continue. [My husband] has allowed me to retain a horse and buggy, and I thank God often for that; hopefully, he will always let me have it.

We had a pure and happy courtship, and started our home with lofty ideals and dreams. God blessed us with a family. But soon after marriage, I found out he did not share the same values as I had thought we did. Slowly this, then that, kept changing and creeping in. Now evening after evening Dad is away from the family, and we often do not know where he is. The computer and internet play a large part in his life. Many a night I have spent alone, crying and praying.

—*Broken in Heart and Spirit*, March 2002

Prayers of a Broken Heart

Help me as I drive to church alone with our little children. Be near me to help explain that Daddy isn't going along. Help me teach them to live for thee. Lead me as I attend family gatherings and weddings and funerals alone, unless I stay home, which is what I wish to do. Help me live as if I were a widow. O God, give me a will to live again even though the zest is gone from my life.

Where is the outstanding young man that people told me is so decent? He grew up in a very unhappy home, but it had seemed to strengthen his faith. My parents approved of him, and told me so before I accepted him, so I believed it was thy will, Lord, for us to marry. He was such a wonderful husband and father—what went wrong? Was it me? Forgive me, Lord, if I caused any part of his discontent.

—*By a sorrowing wife*, August/September 2005

The Y in the Road

Editor's note: This poem was written by a young brother caught in the turmoil of a church that was breaking apart. He uses a Y as a symbol of separation, yet he has not lost hope that the same Y taken backward may yet become a perfect symbol of reconciliation.

> I do not understand why it should be
> That you and I should find
> This Y upon our road and you take one,
> And I the other.
>
> I do not understand why God should lead
> You one way, and me another.
> And yet I feel within my heart
> Though storms should drive our lives apart
> That still you are my brother.
>
> I do not understand and still I hope
> That these two paths we travel
> Will somehow, somewhere merge again
> And come together.
> And then perhaps my weary feet
> Will find new strength and run to greet
> My friend. My brother.

—J. G., November 2011

A Thankful Child

I was a grown child who felt at one time that it was not necessary to live a simple, nonconformed life. I know I caused my parents many heartaches, yet they held to their solid Christian values and continued to teach the simple, godly way without faltering. They gave me many Bible references to read, and my eyes were at last opened.

Because my parents would not give in to my unfaithfulness, their influence at last won me back. But it was more than that. It was their unfailing love as they stood firmly on what they had taught me from childhood. Really, it was God who won. Now I cannot be thankful enough as the days go by, especially when trials come my way.

—*Grateful to my parents*, December 2001

NINE

Clothing

BEING PLAIN MEANS wearing plain clothes, but Amish congregations have varying interpretations of what that means, and this sometimes becomes controversial within the church. So while we may think "all Amish look alike," it is worth going beyond the surface. In our modern world, clothing and fashion make their own statements. Plain clothing largely eliminates individual expression, the need to "look good," peer pressure, being trendy to be accepted, and so on. As Amish women often say, "I don't have to think about what to put on in the morning."

I have often called their way of dress the "Amish uniform," just as many other people around the world have work, school, military, or even religious uniforms. This uniformity in dress identifies individuals with that group, and tells others that they are a member of it. Yet most people don't know why their uniform looks the way it does. I have asked hundreds of students whether they know what their school colors signify on their sports team or band uniforms. Virtually none could tell me.

Likewise, most Amish do not know much of the historical background behind why they wear what they wear. But this "Amish team uniform" makes them highly visible to the modern world around them, and sometimes results in some interesting stories and incidents. These, then, are the words of the people who wear the clothes.

A Plain Purpose

We aren't different simply for the sake of being different. Yet if our dress codes are based on the Christian principles of modesty and health and practicality, we will automatically *be* different from the world.

We need personal convictions against imitating and yearning for the things of the world. Yet this cannot be left entirely up to the individual conscience—it is the church's duty to interpret Bible principles and apply them in ways that are suitable and upbuilding. This includes regulation dress standards. The record of history proves that this is the only effective way to achieve stability and uniformity. No church group has remained free from the bondage of worldly fashions except those who make use of regulation garb.

Plain clothes, however, can be abused. We need to be on our guard lest we become arrogant and self-righteous, and nurture a "holier than thou" attitude because we are a separate people. Humility is a basic Christian virtue. As well, there is no denying that hypocrites can camouflage themselves in plain clothes.

Bishop Daniel Kaufman, a Mennonite writer and church leader of the past, was once asked, "Is there not a danger of people becoming 'clothes Christians'?" His reply was "Yes, but there is a much greater danger of becoming 'clothes worldlings.' I have seen a few of the former but thousands of the latter."

Wearing plain clothes brings accountability. Wherever we go, people interpret our nonconformity as a symbol of genuine religious faith. If anything in our lives is not consistent with faith, we bring shame and reproach not only on ourselves and our church, but also on our Savior, Jesus Christ, whom we represent.

—Joseph Stoll, June 2007

Scriptural Reasons for Plain Dress

The intent of "plain clothes" is to be "not conformed to this world" (Romans 12:2). This nonconformity obviously starts in the Christian's heart, but then will naturally spill over into his outward living, including clothing. It would be hypocritical for the Christian to be "nonconformed" in his heart but "conformed" in his appearance. His actions do not line up with his heart.

Now what is "plain clothing"? In one sense, it is clothing that conventional society and the world all around us declares as *not* its own. They do not always understand "plain clothes," but they do know it represents something dedicated to God.

What does the world define as "plain"? For men it is defined by the plain broad-brimmed hat (not a cowboy hat, baseball cap, office hat, or stocking cap), a full beard (not mustachioed to look like a mountain man or a tough motorcycle gang member, nor stylish and closely trimmed like a professional), suspenders (not the colorful, wide, carpenter kind), and clothing of subdued colors.

For women, "plain" is defined by the traditional pleated head covering (not a hanging veil or a see-through covering), uncut hair, a multilayered cape or apron-type dress (not a vest or a sweater), a long dress (not pants or a skirt). And again as with the men, subdued colors.

The point of being Plain is not to be different for its own sake, but to be consecrated unto Christ, and for others around us to know that is our motive, even if they are not Plain themselves.

Plain clothes challenge the world since the wearer is making a stand for Jesus Christ.

—*One who appreciates plain clothes*, November 2011

Signposts

The ordinance of the devotional covering, or headship veiling, has been subject to abuse and misconceptions. It is commonly referred to as "the cap" or "the white cap." This in itself may not be wrong, provided we understand the significance, not of the covering alone, but of the properly covered head. The devotional covering is to represent obedience to God, subjection to man, modesty, purity, reserve, and piety.

The covering is to have a spiritual connotation. When the emphasis is on having the covering "just so," or if it becomes an ornament to embellish the hair, it is an indication that we have definitely lost sight of the value of the covering as the Lord intended.

Somehow, we tend to think that the larger the covering, the more conservative and pious the people. However, the fact remains, more than anything else, the principle must be alive. In more than one instance, persons being questioned about the covering have replied, "It's a tradition," or "The church requires it."

We have an opportunity to carry a message to the world, often without saying a word. The properly covered head is a sign of a spiritual relationship. It is a token of our acceptance of God's order. It signifies a covenant between us and the Lord, and a personal endorsement of God's arrangement. It quietly rebukes the world's adultery, fashions, and boldness. It speaks of a fondness for the things of God—principles that he has long ago established, and only man has reinterpreted and twisted. How are we presenting that message?

—M. N., December 2013

The Angels That Watch Over Us

The gentle wind rustled among the dry cornstalks in the field on my left as my hurrying feet stirred up the dust of the farm lane. The hill behind me hid our home from view, but in the distance I glimpsed the clump of colorful trees that surrounded my aunts' home. Today was my turn to visit these two elderly ladies and see if they were all right. I was taking a shortcut through the fields, and now came out to a private roadway.

Suddenly, the wild, wide-open roar of three motorcycles shattered the peace of the autumn countryside. As I stepped to the side of the rutted tracks, a blur of men clad in black leather chaps and jackets came speeding toward me. I sighed in relief as the last one passed me, but wait . . .

Deftly, they all turned around and headed toward me again and stopped. Three pairs of eyes riveted upon me, peeking out from behind black masks like portents of evil behind shuttered windows. My heart pounded loudly in my ears. While I stood with leaden feet, rooted with fear, I felt them scrutinizing me from the top of my head to the hem of my long dress. What a world of thoughts and anguish a prayer can encompass in a few moments of time. Just as swiftly as they first appeared, so swiftly they were gone.

They left me shaken and thoroughly convinced that my prayer covering and modest clothing had been a protection to me that day. The prayer veiling is a sign that the woman is in full obedience to God's order of headship. I have heard of evil men admitting that they were kept from harming women by the prayer coverings the women wore. At the same time, this is not saying that harm cannot come to us, even if we are living totally in God's will and wearing the covering.

—Anonymous, May 2004

The Hat: A Religious Symbol?

Early on, men devised portable "roofs" to shield themselves from the elements. The Plain people had little problem with the hat until the styles of the world began to dictate fancy, ornamental hats. Our forefathers responded correctly by requiring a plain, nonconformed hat.

The Industrial Revolution during the nineteenth century created thousands of indoor jobs for men. Soon hats were out of vogue and the fashions of the world began to focus on hairstyles. It soon became apparent that those who had gained "convictions" against the hat also altered their hairstyles to more closely resemble the fashions of the world.

The woman does not wear hers because of rain, heat, or snow—but as a deliberate, visible evidence of her submission to God's order. If she does need protection from the elements or from the dust and grime at work, she wears an *additional* bonnet or protective scarf.

Similarly, when a man wears a hat, the primary purpose is for protection. But it also serves as a token of separation, just like the rest of our plain clothing. It is a religious symbol—but not one of headship. It is a symbol of nonconformity, modesty, and humility. Thus it serves exactly the same purpose for the man as the bonnet or the protective scarf does for the woman.

—J. P. R., August/September 1996

The Fancy Little Dress

Sadie had always been content to dress according to the standards of the church. It was not until she became a mother that temptation came to Sadie in a new and unexpected way, catching her off guard. Sadie was starting to get used to compliments directed at two-week-old Martha.

"It looks like you got a package in the mail today," Marcus said one day as he came into the house.

"It's from Cousin Katie in Pennsylvania," she explained. "She writes that she was making a dress for their little Caroline, so she made one for Martha, too. Isn't it pretty?"

Marcus studied the little pink dress she held up. "Isn't it rather bright?" he asked at length. "Not many people around here would wear that color. Isn't it made in a different way, too?"

Sadie had noticed the fancy stitching and the fullness of the sleeves, but she didn't want to admit it to Marcus. In fact, Sadie had to admit that she wouldn't have made a pink dress at all, much less one like this.

"But it's a gift from Katie," she told herself stubbornly. "If it fits, maybe Martha can wear it to church tomorrow. Besides, there are people in this community who dress their children in clothes just as fancy as this."

On Sunday, the ride to church was silent and Sadie was glad when it ended. Sadie's complacent feeling didn't last long. What was Bishop Dan saying? "We show what is in our hearts by the clothes we put on the innocent little children on our laps," he stated. "We know that children are completely innocent. They don't care if the garments they wear are nearly rags, or the finest that money can buy. It's the mothers and fathers who care. They show, by the way they dress their children, whether their hearts are humble or proud. I always say that children's clothes plainly tell what is in the mother's heart."

Sadie lowered her eyes. Bishop Dan couldn't see her or her baby, but the words were meant for her all the same, even if he didn't know it.

Bishop Dan was not yet finished. "Then we wonder why our young people have such a hard time dressing within the church order, when they grew up from babyhood wearing the fanciest clothes allowed. Then they become teenagers and want to continue dressing as nice as possible, and they have to keep going further and further to accomplish it. But can we blame the teenagers? It seems most of the fault lies in the mother's heart."

Sadie studied little Martha's contented face.

"I'm sorry, Martha, for exposing you to such pride already. It'll be hard enough to raise you in the way you should go, without putting such a stumbling block in your path."

—*A young mother*, October 2002

It Doesn't Matter

It grieves my heart to see this day,
But God must be still sadder
To hear so many people say,
"It doesn't really matter."

Our clothes are sleek, more slick and trim
Than generations gone;
For drift will never say, "enough,"
But beckons on and on.

Though saints of old wore garments plain,
We climb the social ladder;
We're clad for show, prompt to explain,
Just how it doesn't matter.

Hemlines are short, or far too long,
With coverings thin, and perched, and small;
The will is weak, and trends are strong
To dodge the bonnet, hat, and shawl.

With stylish feet, we claim to walk
The straight and narrow way;
With fancy lives and holy talk,
We live not what we say.

Just plain and simple country folks,
The world believes we are;
But we have dropped the ancient yoke;
Our feet have wandered far.

In luxury's shade we dwell at ease;
Our money bags grow fatter;
Our travels take us where we please,
For nothing seems to matter

Too much we copy, one from one,
And unified, we slide
Away from patterns ancient, true,
With Scripture for a guide.

"Woe unto you," the Master said,
"When men speak well, and flatter;"
But we receive the praise of men,
And think it doesn't matter.

Oh, up in arms, ye men of faith
Who love the rugged cross;
Let's turn the tide of worldliness—
The kingdom suffers loss.

Lest in some final, terrible Day
Our lazy dreams may shatter!
For luxury and pride are sin,
And sin does surely matter.
                    —Jonathan Stoll, January 2013

TEN

The World

CHANGE. PROGRESS. We may sometimes use these words interchangeably, but they are not always the same thing. In the modern world, the impact of a change can happen so fast that, if negative, it may be difficult to reverse. The Amish are obviously more cautious about what they adopt from our world. Sometimes they wait long enough to see the results before they decide to accept, adapt, limit, or reject.

Cars make you more mobile and thus break down the community. So for the Amish, the horse culture lives, although they may hire a car and driver for some purposes. Electricity, too, can bring many unwanted and negative influences. Once the house is wired for electricity, the gates have opened. Instead, most of the Amish use bottled gas, compressed air, and hydraulics to operate machinery and appliances.

Yet over the past twenty-five years, many modern inroads have been made, and the most concerning from the Amish perspective is the cell phone. When a phone was just a phone, that was one thing. But now with the internet on your phone, everything is at your fingertips, and some Amish youth even have Facebook accounts. How can you limit what one is exposed to, not to mention its impact? These are questions some non-Amish ask as well, but many Amish feel that the cell phone—referred to as "the world in your pocket"—is the biggest threat to their way of life. Particularly over the past twenty-five years, I have watched this story unfold in the pages of *Family Life*. It is a story we are all a part of: Will we control the technology, or will the technology control us?

On Being Plain

Shocked by a Bowl of Soup

It had been a long day on the train. The January sun had already set as we pulled into the depot in Montreal, Quebec, where we needed to change trains. We had brought along sandwiches and other munchables, but our food was nearly all gone.

"I'd like a bowl of hot soup," my wife said.

"A good idea," I agreed as we lugged our suitcases from the platform and entered the huge terminal thronging with people.

"There is a McDonald's," my wife said, pointing her finger at the familiar arches at one end of the depot.

She stayed with our suitcases while I followed the arrows that led to McDonald's. When I returned I saw that a neatly dressed young man was talking to my wife.

"Are you Amish?" he asked me. "Excuse me for being curious. If you don't want to answer my questions, just tell me to go away. I've read so much about you people, and I admire your values and the principles you stand for. There aren't many people like you left in the world . . ."

"I'll try to answer your questions the best I can," I assured him, feeling a little uneasy because of his flattery, but not wanting to be rude.

"I'm a university student," he said. Then his face grew sober as he hesitated. "I was really quite surprised to see you patronize McDonald's. In fact, I was shocked!"

I smiled, but I could see he was serious. "You see, we've been on the train all day," I told him. "We wanted something hot for supper. To us it's just a place to get something to eat. Why were you shocked by that?"

"Because McDonald's stands for everything you don't!" he said forcefully. Then he changed to other questions, and in a few minutes peered at his watch and excused himself.

The longer I thought about it, the more convinced I became that the young man's concern was not without cause. True, it was not so much the actual food served at McDonald's, but what McDonald's symbolizes in the modern world . . .

Five points of concern

1. The rush-rush syndrome: There are more labor-saving devices than ever before, yet there is no time left over for the really important things in life. People drive faster, but they still don't get home in time to cook a good meal, or to sit down with the family around the table to eat together.

People want their things now and won't wait for them—instant coffee, instant credit, instant communication, instant gratification. It is a day of fax messages, email, computers, internet, microwaves, and automatic appliances.

2. Not a wholesome diet: Although the fast-food giants are becoming more and more health-conscious, still their image continues—serving food that is really not good for you and is popularly labeled as "junk food."

3. All made from the same formula: One secret of success has been mass production, with each hamburger the same as the one before, its content, shape, and size totally predictable. With few exceptions, there is worldwide conformity to the fashions, hairstyles, entertainment, and cultural values that are currently in vogue, and that are spread to the masses by the media of our day.

4. The dollar is ruler over all: In today's world, such multinational giants as Walmart and McDonald's have come to dominate and even to control certain segments of the economy. These companies have become a symbol of a commercialized society where the emphasis is on sales that spell p-r-o-f-i-t.

5. The throwaway spirit: Along with the fast-food industry has come the age of disposables—paper plates, Styrofoam cups, the brown bag, and the hamburger wrapper, all destined for the garbage can after one-time use. We live in a world of throwaways, no doubt the most wasteful generation that has ever lived.

Turning back now to that winter evening in Montreal, I am convinced the curious young stranger saw something that most people overlook. He had a reason to be shocked, not by the bowl of soup itself, but by what it symbolized.

Does that mean I will never again buy a meal at McDonald's? No, for that would be missing the point. But I doubt if I will ever again do so without thinking of what the fast-food industry symbolizes, and how directly opposed this world's values are to ours.

—Joseph Stoll, August/September 2003

Why We Live Simply

Many people measure how successful a person is by how many material possessions he accumulates in his life. But Jesus gave us another rule by which to measure. He said, "A man's life does not consist in the abundance of things he possesses."

We are travelers

The story is told of an Amish farmer who brought a casserole to welcome a new [non-Amish] family moving into a neighboring farmhouse. He helped them unpack one appliance after another—washer, dryer, television, stereo, phonograph, tape deck, compact disc player, computer, dishwasher, coffeemaker, hair dryer, and electric tools.

"If any of these break down," the Amish man said to the newcomers, "please let me know and I'll come over."

"That's very kind of you," they replied gratefully. "Can you fix things?"

"No," said the farmer, "but I can teach you how to live without them."

A consumer-oriented society has taught us to think only negatively of living without things, making us believe that is a misfortune. Why do we do without some of the things that most other people in North America buy and use freely? To understand our thinking about some of these things, we need to keep in mind that we are travelers. Our Master instructed us to despise the things of this world and not permit them to sidetrack us or weigh us down in our journey toward eternity.

Here we are travelers, strangers, and pilgrims, just passing through in search of a better home. If the destination is all-important, it just makes sense to travel lightly. That is one reason we live simply—because we are travelers.

We are neighbors

The second reason we live simply is because we are neighbors. It should make us stop and think when we realize that we are living at a higher standard of luxury than any generation before us in the history of mankind.

How can I live on a level far beyond what I see my neighbor living? How can I live in luxury when my neighbor lacks the necessities? Why do we live simply? We live simply because we are neighbors. Or as someone put it, "We live simply so that others may simply live."

We are disciples

I have kept the most important reason until last—we are disciples. We have a Master whose wishes we seek to honor and follow. When Jesus was here, he left us an outstanding example of simple living. He went about doing good without compromise, rebuking the rich, exposing the hypocrites, healing the sick, and feeding the hungry. He comforted the afflicted and afflicted the comfortable.

Sometimes curious people will look at one particular item we do without and focus on it, trying to figure out what is wrong with it. My wife does not have a dishwasher. We would need to get our house wired. And I don't suppose it would make sense to wire the house just to run a dishwasher. She would surely make good use of a vacuum cleaner, a dryer, a toaster, a blender, a microwave . . . and on and on. All that would likely cost more money—money to buy, money to maintain, and money to power. And so we say no thanks to the dishwasher. There is no convenient stopping place when you are traveling downhill.

Inconsistency is a common objection that people raise toward any attempt to live simply. For example, someone will say, "How can you say something is wrong, and yet you benefit from it? How can you say it is wrong to own a car, and then you turn around and ride in one? I would hate to pay someone to do my sinning for me!"

There are perhaps two misconceptions that need to be cleared up here. First of all, we do not consider modern inventions to be evil in and of themselves. A car, or even a television set, is a material thing. It is the misuse of it that is wrong. With many of the inventions of the past century, we have decided that their potential for harm outweighs their benefit, and have taken measures to restrict their availability to us.

The second misconception we need to address is that if someone does not want to use something a lot, he shouldn't use it at all. Actually, we all do things every day in contradiction of that assumption. An obvious example would be our use of table salt. Without a little we would not remain healthy. Too much will kill us.

—Elmo Stoll, excerpts from October and November 2003

The Swinging Pendulum

In the past twenty or twenty-five years, we as Plain people have experienced something our forefathers never knew—basking in the warmth of favorable public opinion. A generation has grown up among us never having experienced anything different. We have been featured in magazine articles, in movies, and on television. Nearly all of this publicity has been slanted in our favor. People have come to idolize and glorify our way of life, placing us on a pedestal that no humans are worthy of.

Has this been good for us? No, I am afraid not. After all, if we listen to propaganda long enough, we may begin to believe it. Has there been a temptation to take advantage of the special privileges that government officials have tendered to us? Have we stooped to using the Amish name to help sell our products?

Nor should we forget that public opinion can change quickly and very dramatically. We have no guarantee that the present high regard we hold in the public eye is going to continue for very long.

Down through the centuries, there were many who not only suffered persecution but were faithful unto death. As time went on, the idea of what we may call "religious pluralism" came to be accepted more and more. There was greater tolerance for those who differed in their religious beliefs.

And yet there was often an underlying current of looking down on those who were noticeably different. This attitude flared up against German-speaking minority groups during both World War I and World War II, since in each war the Americans were fighting the Germans. Our grandparents and great-grandparents knew what it felt like to be mocked or made fun of, and many young men who were drafted bore the brunt of this anti-German hysteria.

Such scenes seldom occur anymore. Not only is the public better informed now, but there is a friendlier and more receptive attitude. Our reaction to lavish public acclaim? We are not worthy of it. We do not deserve it. It does not belong to us. For if we welcome the world's applause, there can be only one outcome—we will suffer spiritual harm. After all, it is to God that we must give account. It is not the public who will judge us, but the Great Judge over all, and he will judge rightly. Public opinion is a minor thing by comparison.

—Joseph Stoll, January 2006

Church and State

Just Go with the Flow

There are two kingdoms. This is one of the key principles of our Christian faith. The world has its kingdom and its rulers, but Christ has a spiritual kingdom, his Bride, the church.

The New Testament is clear that God's children do have obligations to "the powers that be." Both Romans 13 and our Dordrecht Confession of Faith teach this truth in clearly defined terms. We are to respect and honor the rulers of our government as ordained of God to punish the evil and protect the good. We are to be subject and obedient in all that does not conflict with God's law and kingdom.

We are to pay our taxes. We are to pray for our rulers. And yet our first allegiance is to God's kingdom. Where the two kingdoms clash, the heavenly kingdom has the priority. Our earthly rulers call for patriotism and the defense of one's country, even to the extent of taking the life of a fellow "Christian" if he happens to be a citizen of an enemy country.

How can we maintain clear boundaries in our duties to each of the two kingdoms?

1. In the world's kingdom, the rulers use the "sword" to maintain order, and to control crime. This extends to military force and the waging of war against enemy nations. Christians are to love all men, even their enemies.

2. The chief error of a state church is to include everyone who lives within its political boundaries, whether saint or sinner.

3. The political system of worldly governments is outside the perfection of Christ. Christians therefore should take no part in government offices, in politics, or in voting for candidates. Our duty is to pray for those in authority, and to obey and respect their laws, as long as they do not conflict with our duty to God's kingdom.

4. The world has set up its own social services system for the benefit of its citizens—healthcare insurance plans, welfare programs, schools, disability and [workers'] compensation, old-age pensions, and so on. Christians respect that system, but ought not to be a part of it. Rather, the church has an obligation to care for the needs of its members from the moment of birth to the moment of death. In my lifetime, thankfully, it has come to be generally accepted that it is the church's duty to provide schooling to its children, and not look to the government to provide this.

And yet this is not merely a matter of avoiding negative ties with the world's system. To remain true to our heritage as a people "separated unto God," there are a great many things we need to do in a positive sense. It is when we become luke-warm and worldly-minded that we are vulnerable. The contents of the *Martyrs Mirror* are the accounts of hundreds of faithful Christians who down through the ages had refused to "go with the flow"!

—Joseph Stoll, August 2013

Voting on Our Knees

It seems our people are under pressure as never before to vote. A large ad appears in our local papers under the heading "Amish PAC Voters Project," naming numerous deceptive reasons why Amish should vote, with quotes followed by Amish signatures. Let all be aware that Amish PAC is a worldly political group with an agenda.

For those who are starting to waver, here are a few more things to consider. How are we to know who is the better man, or the right one? To research all the biased, unreliable sources takes something most of us are short on, and that is time. Time we would steal from our family and from the One we vowed to give our all. Or we can blindly vote for the ones "they say we ought."

—Anonymous, December 2020

Beware of Slandering

"The country is in a terrible mess."

"The politicians have no idea what they're doing."

"How stupid can they get?"

"We will be completely ruined if nothing changes."

The above remarks I hear constantly, and it scares me. For it is our own people who are speaking. It is not the ruin of our country that scares me as much as the fact that we are so involved in politics. We slander those in authority. We think we are smarter and better than they. We say these things to non-Amish neighbors, and it can't be a light to them.

Slandering is plainly forbidden in the Scriptures. This means disrespect shown to anyone, not just our church brethren. I am reminded of the saying "As long as you think you're better than someone else, you aren't."

Our forefathers left their homes in Europe to come to America so they could worship as their conscience led them. We still have this privilege. Instead of appreciating our freedom of today, we worry about tomorrow. It is not wrong to stay informed about what is happening out there if we do it in a godly way. Let's pray for our government, and trust God for the future.

—*Anonymous in New York*, November 2020

Technology and Cell Phones

As you read these selections, notice the years they were written along with the concerns expressed.

The Battle Continues

The aged bishop was battle-weary and full of years. Telephones, electricity, tractor farming, running water, stylish dress, various gadgets and appliances for the home, computers—each had generated its share of controversy over the years.

To him, the cell phone was a real cause for concern—perhaps in a class with the radio, television, and the computer. Happily for him, the church had been fully supportive in these other issues, though there had always been some members who had challenged the church's stand.

Of late, however, there was fresh cause for alarm. He had been hearing rumors, "Minister So-and-So thinks cell phones are harmless and should be allowed." "Bishop So-and-So is agreed to allow them now that they are available in a plain-Jane phone—no extra features, no camera, no memory, no voicemail, no calculator, and so on."

The old man had recently read an editorial in which the writer had lamented how much the cell phone had become a modern-day idol. If only people would treasure their Bible as they do their cell phone! We would carry it with us, and time and again we would get it out to study the messages and to talk with God. And if the unthinkable happened, that we forgot to take it along when we left home, surely we would turn around quickly and retrieve it!

—Anonymous, January 2009

A Fire in the Land

The computer and its sister, the cellular phone, are changing many things in the business world, the entertainment world, and society in general. The modern outlook focuses on man's inventions as a means to make life easier and better.

Today the cell phone, the regular computer, and wireless laptop computers are becoming increasingly similar to each other. Using one serves as an introduction to using the others. As these various machines have become more readily available, using any of them draws toward the use of the internet.

Why is the internet so enticing? Because it is the central focus of all communication and knowledge in the world today. This puts you on a slippery slope to get in deeper and deeper. This is the very essence of this electronic technology—there are no stops, no limits, no end.

Following is a list of principles and practical suggestions that will help us resist the pressure:

1. Keep the scale of operations small enough so we can do without this technology.
2. A belief, based on Scripture, that cross-bearing, toil, and labor are intertwined with a common, nonconformed lifestyle as Christians.
3. A respect for church standards that are well defined (*Ordnung*), and a respect for the church's leadership.
4. A nonelectronic outlook and approach to life.
5. A willingness to suffer to maintain a safe standard, based on Scripture.
6. United support from the brotherhood to find alternatives.
7. Abstaining from becoming familiar with the use of computers.
8. Leaders and members not excusing their accountability in this.

Many Plain churches are at a crossroads today. To discourage computers and yet tolerate them is the language of trying to appease the two sides.

Some secular writers have referred to the electronic revolution as a fire that is sweeping the land. Fire consumes all that is in its path. Can we embrace this fire and allow it to enter our midst and not be burned?

—*An Amish minister*, April 2010

"Celling" Our Heritage: Cell Phones, Plain People, and the Electronic Age

"Watch your step!" the conductor admonished cheerfully. In the waiting area we arranged our luggage and settled down to wait. Looking around at my fellow travelers, something struck me again that I had noticed on the train . . . almost everyone was occupied. People were on their cell phones, sending and receiving text messages, watching movies on their laptop computers, playing games, or listening to music.

Cell phones have entered some congregations by way of construction crews. Broadfalls are an old style of trousers, but many of them today carry sleek and modern phones. No decision was made (except by default), no agreement was reached, and yet in many Amish communities a very important bridge has been crossed. Should we accept a major advance like this with little thought? History paints a disheartening picture of churches who embraced every new thing that came along.

Some Amish and Mennonite churches said no thanks to the horseless carriage, but others saw no reason to worry. Objects are not "good" or "bad" in themselves, they reasoned. The important thing was to use them right.

The *World Book Encyclopedia* says:

> The automobile revolutionized the American way of life and changed living patterns. . . . Probably no other invention, discovery, or technological advance has created greater or more rapid changes in society. . . . The automobile influences where people live and work and how they spend their leisure time . . .

The decision to "go modern" brought far-reaching social change that ultimately did have a spiritual effect. Limiting the use and type of vehicles lessens the destructive effects of easy mobility on community living. We should turn down cell phones for the very same reasons. It makes no logical sense to reject cars and accept cell phones.

—Jonathan Stoll, November 2012

Bondage Is the Issue

This past summer while traveling by bus, in front of us sat a lad who had a smartphone in his pocket. Without even trying to, we could see that he was searching under the heading "Men Wanting Women." It was shocking what came up on the screen.

But what was really sad was the way he took out his phone and did a search, then returned the phone to his pocket. Then time and again, hour after hour, he would take out his phone and look once more. Here was a young lad who obviously had an addiction.

We had to think of people who feel sorry for us Amish, convinced that we are "bound by traditions" while they in the world are "free." To us, this addiction to the cell phone appeared as being bound in the true sense of the word.

We may try to convince ourselves that we wouldn't use the extras, but very few people are strong enough to withstand temptations like that. The further away we can stay, the safer we are.

—Mark and Dora Stoll, January 2013

The Point of No Return?

With all the changes being accepted among us, the smartphone must be the deadliest. Any child with a smartphone has immediate access to every movie and every song in this world, along with pornography, video games, social media, and unlimited information on everything from making drugs to committing suicide.

Nomophobia, the fear of not being able to use your smartphone device [an abbreviated form of "no-mobile-phone phobia"], is becoming a worldwide epidemic. Phone addiction is on the rise. Just temporarily restricting teenagers from their cell phone has caused severe depression and anxiety attacks and maimed their ability to communicate face-to-face.

The smartphone is instant weather reports for the roofer or farmer. It has good answers to hundreds of inquiries. It is a useful tool for an honest man, but it is also the devil's playground for a weak individual, or for immature children and teenagers.

If we continue as we have, we are headed downhill. The longer it goes, the faster our wagon will coast. I can only pray that my children's children will have enough foresight to look ahead for an exit, and the strength to veer their coasting wagon off before it hits the bottom.

—N. S., Indiana, April 2019

City Lights

In olden days the neon lights
Attracted boys to sin's delights.
Today the worldly lights are seen
Emitted from a dancing screen.

The screen is held by eager hands.
It draws the boys to sinful lands,
Addictions grab by drink and drug,
But internet's a bigger thug.

The world is reached with all its doom
In office, car, or living room.
Let's give a church that's nourishing,
Where holiness is flourishing.

—Benjamin Zaiger, November 2019

At the Gates of Sodom

Social media connects people. At an impulse, if I am plugged in to social media, I can make a comment, take a picture, or even take a video, and instantly send it to dozens of people. I can send a text to someone who is sitting a few rows ahead of me in the church pews. (That certainly happens.) Am I saying that all young men who carry a smartphone would do these things? No, I am not saying that. But I am saying that the unfiltered internet is like playing with fire.

Keeping out the enemy with filters is like putting up a woven wire fence to stop the wind. It is not a solution that thinking Christians will choose. Besides, they do not even eliminate the problem of wasted time, social media addiction, and distraction from the real world.

Should our young people have smartphones? No, young people should have no access whatsoever to smartphones. (Neither should their parents.)

By accepting smartphones, we are throwing on the garbage heap several principles on which our fathers took a stand before us. They said no to the radio and recorded music. Shall we take on a device that brings us a thousand choices in music? They did not allow cameras. Shall we accept a device that has not only a camera but a video camera? They would have given their lives before they would have installed a television set in their living room. Shall we allow our sons and daughters to have a device that brings all of television and much more into their bedroom?

There is wrong teaching that says Christians must learn to use these inventions rightly. But God will not protect us from temptations if we willingly walk into them.

—*An Amish minister*, August/September 2020

* * *

Please Let Me Stay

As the snow falls gently, my spirit soars to new heights. I reflect on the past events of my life, having rehearsed them again and again to my children at Christmastime. Last year, sixteen-year-old John said, "Daddy, you must write down your story so your grandchildren can read it after you are gone." So after much thought, I wrote out by hand the following account . . .

I was born on the South Side of Chicago on November 10, 1960. *Home* was a word I knew belonged to the English language, but I did not understand what it really meant. I lived on a street whose name I do not remember, in one of the row houses with numbers beginning with 205 to 210. Each bed was full every night and sometimes the living room floor held the overflow. Each night I would go to one of the houses until I found a place to lie down.

I knew who my mother was, but I rarely saw her, and I do not remember having much feeling for her. I am not sure even yet as to what my last name is. Mom said my name was "W. M.," but I was never told what it stood for

I don't know who supplied the food, but I know my mom and other mothers brought in food from time to time. I was glad when I was old enough to go to school. They had a program for children who were poor to arrive early and get something warm to eat for breakfast.

I had one pastime. I loved to read. My second-grade teacher introduced me to the world of books. During the month of November, I checked out a book that contained a story about an Amish home that had all the family together on Christmas Day. I read it again and again. Family . . . family.

Then I began to dream. If only I could live in a home like that. A group of them lived east of Chicago in northern Indiana about a hundred miles away. So I decided, "Over Christmastime, I am going to an Amish home just like those in the book."

I left the row houses of Chicago on December 22, 1969. I took the bus east through Chicago as far as I could. I spent the first night at the bus station, pretending that I was going to take the bus the next morning.

My plan was to get a ride with a trucker that was going east. Finally, I went outside to pick a truck in which to stow away. One was unlocked. I hurriedly crawled into the big rig and made my way into the area behind the seat.

How long we had been driving, I did not know. I knew I had to make my getaway as soon as the driver left the rig. As soon as I opened the door, I could tell it was snowing hard and had gotten colder. I had to hurry, for I didn't want to get caught, but I hurried too fast. When my foot landed on the second step, I slipped and fell.

When it was all over, I was upside down with my head, shoulders, and arms in the snow and my left foot caught on something on the passenger side of the truck. I called out, "Please, someone help me!" I started to dream about a warm stove, hot food, laughing children, and happy sounds.

Somewhere in my dream I faintly heard sirens and felt myself being lifted onto a bed with voices asking, "Who is he?" I heard them ask me, "Who are you?" All I could think to say was, "Amish . . . Amish . . . Amish."

As I slowly woke up, I was aware of the activity around me. "We do not know who he is. As he was being brought to the hospital, he kept saying, 'Amish.' We have called for some Amish to come to see if we can unravel this mystery."

Two men walked in, and they looked just like those in the pictures in the book. "Hello, I am Mrs. Joyce Barr, social worker with the state of Indiana. We do not know who he is, but he kept saying, 'Amish' while being transported to the hospital in the ambulance."

Mrs. Barr shook her head in bewilderment. "What are we to do? There is nothing wrong with him, and no one to pay the bill. Mr. and Mrs. Henry Yoder are approved for foster care, and they are Amish. Do you think they would take the boy until we can decide what to do?"

The one bearded man said, "Yes, I believe they would be willing."

Now they noticed that I was fully awake, and Mrs. Barr began to question me. "What is your name?" she asked.

"W. M." That was all I could say.

Mrs. Barr took me to the Henry Yoder home in her car. What happened the next few days seemed like a whirl in my head. By then, it was the 24th of December. I barely remember eating supper. The chatter and the love filled my very being with emotions I never had before. Soon I was fast asleep from exhaustion because of all that had taken place.

We woke up early on Christmas Day. They asked me if I wanted to help do chores. It was all fun to me—new sights of cows, pigs, chickens, and milk.

The morning was spent getting ready for the family to be together. Henry said we would bow our heads in prayer. I bowed my head in prayer, not knowing for sure how to pray. My prayer went something like this: "Dear Lord, please let me stay here forever."

It was just too much for this heart of mine. I began to cry . . . and not just cry, but sob and shake. Henry got up from his chair, came over to mine, and picked me up with two strong arms and carried me to the rocking chair by the stove.

While holding me, he began to rock slowly, and with his deep voice he said, "Family, sing 'Joy to the World' as W. M. settles down." After the last verse, Henry said, "It just dawned on me that W. M. must stand for 'wise men.' I believe W. M. is like the wise men of long ago who came from far away in search of Jesus, and found him."

Henry Yoder and his wife adopted me two years after my arrival. I always felt it a privilege to be a part of their family. They gave the name of William Melvin Yoder to me. The years have rolled along, and I am now in my fifties. I married an Amish girl named Miriam and we have five boys and two girls. Of course, we named our first boy Henry and our first girl Mary.

Today, as a father and grandfather, I feel a great burden as we live in this modern world with all the many choices we have to make. Many years ago, as a little boy, I left the South Side of Chicago in search of a better life. Tell me, why do the boys and girls of our Plain churches leave their Anabaptist heritage in search of a worldly life? I sob at times, as I did that day many years ago, when I think about what they are throwing away.

I pray that when I leave this earth and am ushered into the presence of our Lord and Savior, Jesus Christ, he will honor my request when I ask him, "Let me stay, dear Lord, please let me stay."

—W. M. Y., December 2013

ELEVEN

Aging, Illness, and Death

AS I CARED FOR MY MOTHER for several years before she died, ultimately placing her in a nearby facility when I could no longer care for her myself, my assessment of how the Amish treat and care for the elderly certainly changed. I had a renewed appreciation for a community where the elderly are valued, where there are no "nursing homes," and where adult children take care of their parents, often in a separate addition to the main house. And when necessary, the entire community helps with medical bills or other needs. I found accounts from caregivers both moving and humbling. When I visited my mother each day, I would see women in wheelchairs stuck in front of a television, older folks who rarely saw their family and had limited contact with others. I came to respect the Amish way even more. It is certainly not perfect, but perhaps we could learn a few things from their view of illness, aging, and death.

Essence of Life

> The wrinkled hand holds the tiny one;
> The nearly done and the just begun,
> The very old and the very young,
> 'Tis the course of life, so short—so long.
> The white head bends to the wee one fair,
> And the essence of time is captured there.
>
> A portrait of life in a glance is seen,
> The aged, the babe, and the years between.
> The dawn meets dusk, and their beauty glows,
> Together—the bud and the fading rose.
> Both rest in the hands of a God unseen,
> The young—and the old—and the years between.

Author's note: Only six weeks after this poem was written, my grandmother was called home. I treasure the memory of seeing her cuddle our newborn daughter in her frail arms.

—M. J. Z., August/September 2005

The Place of "Old People" in the Church

We all know that without young people, the church would soon die out. But what about the elderly? What place do we fill in the church? Are we still needed? Moreover, how can we possess a wholesome view of aging and death?

The old saying is very true, "The young *can* die, but the old know that they soon *must*." Not everyone is granted a lengthy autumn, but as the years flow by one after the other, the certainty of approaching death becomes more and more real.

Throughout the Bible, old people are held up for veneration. Old age is not something to dread, but the culmination of a fruitful life, in which grandchildren crown the twilight days (see Proverbs 17:6).

But it is in the apostle Paul's letter to Titus that we find the clearest instructions for older Christians, and are reminded how great their responsibility is to be a good example and to teach those who are younger.

First is the message to the men, "That the aged men be sober, grave, temperate, sound in faith, in charity, in patience" [Titus 2:2]. We must be a good example to the younger brethren. We older men are to be a positive influence in the church, role models for those who follow in our footsteps, ready to give encouragement and counsel to those who desire it, as well as correction and reproof in a spirit of humility and love.

Then Paul directs Titus concerning the conduct of the aged women, but with an added note to be "teachers of good things" [v. 3]. The older sisters are to teach the young women by word and example to be sober, to love their husbands, to love their children, to be discreet, chaste, keepers at home, good, obedient to their own husbands.

With God's blessings, the sunset years can be among the most fruitful and rewarding of one's life.

—Joseph Stoll, November 2009

Caregivers

Honor Your Father and Mother

We live with my parents on my homeplace. Grandfather soon got a job and worked away from home while Grandmother busied herself with making quilts, tending garden, and helping her daughters.

As our family grew, more adjustments were necessary. It was during these years that both parties developed one of the basic rules toward a peaceful environment where two families share one roof. We learned to respect one another. My wife learned to respect her mother-in-law for who she was. Grandmother also learned to appreciate her daughter-in-law for who she was. They both had their own kitchen in which they each did their work according to their own taste. It is very important when two families live in one place that they all learn to mind their own business. This also applies to the men. The balance between giving advice and meddling in other people's matters is not always easily established, even within families.

The role of order with the children can become complex with four adults in the home. The order we developed was that "Doddys" [grandparents] were in charge of the children when we were not around, but when we were present those roles shifted to us as parents.

It is very sobering to watch the aged grow week and feeble, because we are also following their steps. They must surrender first this, and then that. Aged people are just as human as young people, and giving up does not necessarily become easier with age. The only difference is that the aged see more clearly that their time on earth will soon be over, and we do well if we also learn that lesson today.

—*For Love in the Home*, October 1995

My Aged Aunt

I see our hands together often. I take her hands to lift her from her bed. I hold her hands to lead her to her chair. I help her wash her hands at the sink. Her hands are frail and mine are firm. And I look at our hands together, and think of what all her hands have done.

They have known the strain of hard labor and the weariness of long hours. They have put away many jars full of vegetables and innumerable shelves of fruit. They have shelled peas and peeled potatoes and chopped onions. I like to look at her hands.

They have eased the load of many mothers and cradled with care many babies not her own. They have been clasped in prayer and offered in service.

But now they are old. Her fingers are long and wrinkled. Her nails are cracked and yellow. I take her hands in mine and look at ours together. They are a study in contrasts. Her hands are limp and mine are lithe. Her hands clench sometimes in confusion, and my hands move as I bid them. I look at her cracked nails and my smooth ones. I study her crooked fingers and my straight ones. I compare her wrinkled ninety-year-old hands and my firm nineteen-year-old ones.

And it is my prayer that someday my hands will be as beautiful as hers.

—S. J. Lehman, June 2005

Most Educational Days

We have had the privilege to be caregivers within our home for years, also days at a time in other homes, some of which lengthened into years. If someone would ask me which were the most educational days of my life, I would be quick to reply they were my days as a caregiver.

Now that I am older and the tables have been turned and I have had others wait on me at times, my thoughts are drawn to the following poem, "Beatitudes for Friends of the Aged."

> Blessed are they who understand
> My faltering step and palsied hand.
> Blessed are they who know my ears today
> Must strain to catch the things they say.
> Blessed are they who seemed to know
> That my eyes are dim, and my wits are slow.
> Blessed are they who looked away
> When my tea was spilled at the table today.

Blessed are they with a cheery smile
Who stopped to chat for a little while.
Blessed are they who never say,
"You've told that story twice today."
Blessed are they who know the ways
To bring back memories of yesterdays.
Blessed are they who make it known
That I'm loved, respected, and not alone.
Blessed are they who ease the days
On my journey Home, in loving ways.

—*A Faithful* Family Life *Reader*, March 2000

Lessons from Ida Mae

I was one of the fortunate few who had the privilege of attending Ida Mae's "classroom." All of us "pupils" who went to her school learned to love our teacher dearly. Her methods of teaching were very different from the usual. During the two years I attended Ida Mae's school, there were few spoken words from our teacher.

Let me explain. Instead of having desks, a blackboard, and educational posters on the wall, Ida Mae's "classroom" had a hospital bed, a wheelchair, and a hydraulic lift along with other sickroom items. She was a victim of Alzheimer's disease.

Ida Mae taught us *contentment*. She ate what we spooned into her mouth, and then made herself as comfortable as she could and dozed until we put her back into bed several hours later.

She taught us *forgiveness* by forgiving. While pushing her from her small bedroom to the kitchen, I would accidentally bump her foot or leg. When I would tell her I'm sorry, she responded by waving her hand, a look of forgiveness on her face, as if saying, "That's okay. That's nothing."

Daily, Ida Mae taught us *unselfishness*. When we fed her, she always wanted us to eat some of what we were feeding her. If we offered her a drink, she often said, "You may have some first." If we stood beside her, she often pointed to a chair.

There was the memorable Sunday, just months before she left us, that she taught me the true meaning of *compassion*. A dear friend and I were staying with her while the rest had gone to church. I began to tell my friend of the great sadness, the deep sorrow my husband and I were going through.

I was not aware of how close I was sitting to Ida Mae, or of her presence, until I felt her gentle touch on my shoulder. I looked up into her face. Her eyes were so sad, her face completely filled with compassion. Her hands were folded as in prayer as she held them up to me, nodding her head wordlessly.

"Oh, yes, Ida Mae. Thank you for reminding me that prayer is the answer." She again nodded her head, still holding her folded hands toward me.

Ida Mae's classroom doors have now closed. She left us early one spring morning after a lingering illness that lasted longer than anyone expected. We can never be her pupils again. We will always cherish, always treasure the precious opportunity to learn in Ida Mae's "classroom."

—*An assistant caregiver*, January 2015

A Place in the Sun

Who will take Grandma? Who will it be?
All of us want her, I'm sure you'll agree.
Let's call a meeting; let's gather the clan;
Let's get it settled as soon as we can.
In such a big family, there's certainly one
Willing to give her a place in the sun.

Remember the days when she was so spry,
Baked her own cookies and made her own pie?

She helped with our lessons and mended our seams;
Kissed away troubles and minded our dreams.
Wonderful Grandma, we all love her so.
Isn't it dreadful she's no place to go?

Strange how we thought she'd never wear out,
But see how she walks; it's arthritis, no doubt.
Her eyesight has failed her; her memory is dim;
She's apt to insist on the silliest whim.
When people get older they become such a care.
Yes, she must have a home, but the question is, where?

One little corner is all she would need;
A shoulder to cry on, her Bible to read.
A chair by the window, the sun coming through;
Some pretty spring flowers all covered with dew.
Who'll warm her with love so she won't mind the cold;
Oh, who will take Grandma, now that she's old?
—Anonymous, August/September 1993

A Community Comes Together

When caring for my father's needs at night became too much for my brother, the other men in the family helped out, one night a week each. That meant driving twelve or fourteen miles one way with horse and buggy for some of them. Neighbors filled in the remaining nights since there were fewer sons than days of the week.

After Father died, the children took turns keeping Mother in their own homes for one or two months at a time. Her mental health abilities no longer matched her physical ones, so it took a lot of patience and quick thinking to care for her in a loving way. And love is a very essential ingredient when caring for those who can no longer care for themselves.

Two years passed, and then it was decided it would be easier to have the sisters come care for mother than to move her. For nearly eight more years, the family cared for her in this way. Each one took a day and a night, and no neighbors were needed. After Mother stayed in one place all the time, her mind did not deteriorate so fast anymore. We all need a sense of security.

At present there are five old people in our district who need help in one way or another. Three of them need care day and night, one during the day only, and one only at night. This gives you an idea of what one community is doing for those who can no longer care for themselves.

—Anonymous, March 2000

Aging and Death

Farewell to a Good Friend

Recently, death parted us from an aunt by marriage in our former home community. The funeral was planned for Sunday, so my wife and I left at noon the day before.

We arrived at Uncle's home shortly after seven o'clock. The house was almost full of people—besides the children and grandchildren there were neighbors, relatives, and friends. Because one son was handicapped, my uncle and his wife had learned to know many people with the same experience. Visiting was going on in hushed tones. It is in such a place that friends meet, acquaintances are renewed, and relatives who have not seen each other for years are reunited.

As we were leaving after a short stay, the words of Ecclesiastes 7:2–4 came to my mind: "It is better to go to the house of mourning, than to go to the house of feasting: for that is the end of all men; and the living will lay it to his heart. . . . The heart of the wise is in the house of mourning; but the heart of fools is in the house of mirth."

The next morning we returned to the departed's home for the funeral. It was held as all Amish funerals are held (though slight variations are seen from settlement to settlement). In the main house the family was seated first, followed by the brothers and sisters, then the in-laws, nephews and nieces, cousins, and so on. Everyone present had the opportunity to hear a funeral sermon, which lasted about an hour and a half. The time was divided among three ministers.

Following the usual tradition, the first minister spoke about the creation and the fall of man. Once again we were reminded that man was created to live eternally, but after the fall of man, death became the penalty for sin, and now *all men must die.*

The second sermon was preached by an older minister, a neighbor and close friend of our uncle, the two having lived in the same neighborhood all their lives. He spoke much about the resurrection and final judgment. His message was especially touching because his own wife had passed away within the past year.

The home bishop preached the final sermon. We were admonished that we need not mourn as those who have no hope, and were reminded that we did not come to the funeral to help the departed sister. Death is the door between this life and eternity, and once we have passed through that door, the day of grace and repentance is past.

After we had knelt for prayer, the obituary was read, and then everyone filed past the open coffin for a last viewing. Psalm 90 was read during this time, with those familiar words once more comparing our fleeting years to a timeless eternity.

After the services, those who chose to traveled the half mile to the cemetery to attend the funeral. Most of us walked and enjoyed the mild March day. Arriving at the cemetery, we paused and peered into the open grave. This always gives me a feeling I cannot put into words. Someday, if the Lord tarries, a similar grave will be my body's destination.

After a short while the body arrived, and a hush fell over those already there. When the family was ready, the coffin was carried to the grave, with the close relatives following. The coffin was placed over the grave, supported by two poles that had been fashioned for the purpose. Next, straps were positioned below, the poles were removed, and the body was gently lowered to its resting place. The lid of the "rough box" was put into place, and then the four pallbearers stood back, shovels in hand, ready for the signal to begin filling the grave.

The bishop read two lines of the familiar hymn "Gute Nacht, ihr meine Lieben" ("Good Night, My Beloved Ones"), and about a dozen men started singing. The thud of the first shovels of dirt hitting the wooden vault was again heard, a stark reminder that we are dust, and to dust we must return.

After the grave was filled, the bishop spoke the final words, saying we have now gone as far as we can with the body of our departed sister, having committed it back to the earth until "the Lord himself shall descend from heaven with a shout . . ." (1 Thessalonians 4:16–18).

After the Lord's Prayer was observed in silence, the ceremony was over. We turned from the new grave and strolled through the graveyard, reliving memories of former neighbors, friends, and relatives who have been laid to rest here since the cemetery was started twenty years ago.

Afterward we returned to our uncle's home for a light lunch and a short afternoon of fellowship. We visited with friends and relatives we seldom see, the former neighbors and boyhood chums I had not met for twenty-five years.

The next morning we returned home. We had parted with a dear friend, and it left an empty spot in our hearts. At the same time we had once more been reminded of the end we, too, will someday face. We had again committed to our hearts the uncertainty of life and the fact that someday we must leave our earthly possessions behind and meet our Maker.

—Yost N. Miller, December 1996

Lament of a Senior Citizen

I am sitting alone at the window,
Feeble and old and gray . . .
Sitting alone by the window,
Longing for callers today.

So many weeks have been passing,
And nobody comes to chat.
Have they forgotten I'm living?
No, it surely cannot be that.

Just now the thought has struck me:
"When I was young, did I
Go visit and cheer the shut-ins?"
(I heave a great big sigh.)

I'm afraid I was often too busy,
Wrapped up in my personal stuff.
It took too much time and effort,
And I just didn't care quite enough.
So here I still am sitting,
Passing the time away,
Sitting alone by the window
Longing for callers today.

—D. M., July 1993

How One Girl Met Her Grandpa

The kitchen is bright and tidy. At the end of the table sits an old man with bushy white eyebrows, thin white hair, and a sparse beard. His granddaughter thinks he looks fierce. She sits to his left and watches him carefully, as a four-year-old will. The little girl begins to notice that there is something odd about Grandpa. Auntie has to remind him to keep on eating, and a couple of times she has to stop him from doing rather childish things, such as pouring water onto his plate or taking too much jam.

The girl learns as she grows older that her grandfather suffered from Alzheimer's disease. Then she understands. The stranger they had visited was in a sense someone else. She would never have the privilege of meeting the real Grandpa.

But the girl was wrong. As the years passed, she was able to meet him again and again.

The first place she was able to meet her grandpa was in school. In vocabulary class she learned the meaning of the word *earnest*: "serious and intense, not joking; zealous and sincere." Her grandfather's name had been Ernest, and her teacher was Ernest's youngest son. The teacher talked about his father in class. He related many stories of his growing-up years, and how his father had reprimanded him when he got into mischief.

Another place the girl met her grandpa was through his brothers and sisters who were still living. As the girl got to know her grandpa better, she began to see him in her youngest brother. Her brother was quiet and deliberate. He talked in a voice so low you almost had to lean forward to hear him. He shook silently when he laughed.

Finally, she learned more about her grandfather's earliest years. His parents had died when he was still young, and he had become the man of the home at a tender age. She heard about the death of his sister and his brother, and then later of Grandpa's firstborn child. She knew Grandma had died of cancer, leaving Grandpa a widower.

So now, if someone asks her if she remembers her grandfather, she hesitates and does not know just what to say. "Yes," she might answer, "he died when I was seven." But then she would like to explain that she never really knew him before he died. She only met him afterward.

Editor's note: The author of this touching article is a member of the Old Order River Brethren and lives in Lancaster County, Pennsylvania.

—Karen Conley, June 2001

Drawing a Heart

After our son left us so suddenly in a farm accident, the word *family* was very difficult for me to write. It just felt like we were no longer a family and never would be. But time has a way of healing. You learn to live with your loss.

Sometimes when I want to sign all the children's names on a greeting card or something, I would like to also include our deceased son's name but feel that I shouldn't. One mother told me she would draw a heart where the child's name would have been. People who don't know about her loss won't realize why the heart is there; those who know will understand.

—*A Pennsylvania Mother*, March 1994

A Widow's Life

How lonely is a widow's life—
She can no longer hear
Her husband's step, her husband's voice,
Which brought such love and cheer.

No meals to cook, no clothes to clean,
The hours seem long and drear,

My life has changed so very much,
Without his presence near.

So empty is his bed and chair,
And as the night draws near,
The tears fall fast as prayers are said—
His voice just is not here.
It seems so hard when Sunday comes
To go alone to church.
The men file in, but for his face
There is no use to search.

I hope that you with husbands dear,
Will treat them lovingly;
Because someday (it may be near)
With you they may not be.

—Mrs. Levi L. Schlabach, November 1995

The Tragedy at Nickel Mines

If we look back and review the past year, who of us does not think of the tragic event on October 2 at an Amish school in Lancaster County, Pennsylvania? I cannot think of any parallel, at least in recent years, that was so widely publicized and that caused such shock waves as this sad happening.

We at Pathway received a number of letters from as far away as California and England expressing sympathy for the grieving families and asking for an address so they could write to them. From among this mail, we have selected the following to share with our readers.

From Jim Blubaugh, a Protestant minister in West Virginia:

Monday, October 2, 2006, dawned like so many other days in Nickel Mines, Pennsylvania. The members of the Amish community were already busy with their chores before the autumn sun drove away the darkness of night.

A hearty breakfast, and the children made their way to the one-room school. Their day had scarcely begun when an intruder entered their school. The acts of cruelty that he had planned would never have entered the minds of the students or their families.

The police arrived minutes after being notified, but the horror had already begun. Ten innocent girls—five dead and five seriously wounded. And to end his plot, the sinister character took his own life. Everyone was voicing the same question, "Why?" But no one had an answer

Nickel Mines—indeed America itself—will never be the same. Heroes were not born that day; they were simply revealed. A policeman clinging to the lifeless body of a little girl. An older child offering herself first in a futile attempt to save the younger ones. A community pulling together in a time of tremendous need. An Amish group visiting the home of the [killer's family] and expressing forgiveness.

May we recognize the real visitor at Nickel Mines— forgiveness. Forgiveness at a time when it is not even humanly possible to forgive.

—Joseph Stoll, December 2006

On Illness and Injury

A Grateful Receiver

We were young farmers, struggling to cope with falling milk prices and high feed costs. And two months earlier, my husband had been in an accident. While his injuries were not life-threatening, they were major enough to put him off work for several months. Two surgeries had been needed. He was healing—praise God, he was healing!

The church had already offered to take care of the main hospital bill. The beauty of a brotherhood of believers was driven home as never before. But doctor visits had to be paid somehow, some way. Taxi drivers. Extra hired help. Medications.

And then the envelopes began to show up in our mailbox. Always, they were plain and thin with no return address, and our own address printed in simple, block lettering. Some held a single hundred-dollar bill. Others held two or three. One had six. Yet the envelope containing a lone twenty-dollar bill meant no less. Someone cared enough to send what they could.

The envelopes did not all come by mail. Some were found tucked into a drawer under a stack of folded towels. Or in a milkhouse cabinet.

It wasn't limited to money. Boxes of groceries found their way to our home. Kind neighbor ladies brought ready-made meals. Taxi drivers took us to doctor visits at reduced rates. Neighbor boys helped with chores. Siblings and friends came to help with whatever needed doing. Two of the neighboring farmers stocked our horse barn with enough corn fodder to last the winter.

And we wondered . . . how will we ever repay all these generous, helpful people? Sometimes we gave voice to the question. Always, the reply carried the same message, "Pass it on. You need not repay us, but someday, when you are able to do so, please pass it on."

—R. S., November 2015

Brighter Days Ahead

My mother struggled with mental illness off and on for many years. She raised a large family. My father, dear as he was, might not have been as much help with the family as he could have been, so that caused additional stress for her.

She was such a dear mother and her love for her family knew no bounds.

I remember during my growing-up years how my heart just ached for Mother when she was feeling blue, with no will to work or even to live. Normally, she was a very active person, making every minute count. You could feel her breakdowns coming beforehand—sensing it, dreading it, yet feeling helpless. She was by nature a talkative person, but during these moods she became quiet, fearful of being left alone, and worrying unnecessarily over the smallest things.

For many years now she has been free of this illness. God's grace and mercy pulled us through those difficult times. It brought us closer to God and helped us have understanding and compassion for others who are afflicted in similar ways.

—Anonymous, April 1993

Dealing with Dementia

Grandma Troyer has dementia. As a result, she no longer always thinks and talks logically. She lives with her son and his family. At first the Troyers found it difficult to deal with this "new" Grandma who said and did such strange things, but they have learned a few lessons that make it easier.

If she says "Yesterday a whole boatload of Indians sailed down the river past my window," they may reply with "That's interesting. How many were there?" They have learned there is no use arguing. In Grandma's mind, it really happened.

One evening at the supper table, Grandma suddenly pushed her plate over to Dad. "Will you cut my pancake?" she wondered.

Dad looked at the "pancake" on Grandma's plate. What he saw was a round hot pad, slathered with butter and drizzled with honey. There was no way to hide the mistake from Grandma, so he chose instead to make her laugh about it. "I'm afraid I can't cut it either," he said. "It's a hot pad."

"Well!" exclaimed Grandma. "Whatever is wrong with me?" Then she burst into peals of laughter, and everyone laughed with her. They were glad Grandma still had her sense of humor!

—*"Lena," a caregiver*, June 2018

TWELVE

Controversies

THE READER HAS SEEN BY NOW that the Amish certainly do not agree on everything. There are often strongly worded discussions and outright disagreements in the pages of *Family Life*, yet the editors always request respect and arguments backed up by more than mere emotion. These controversies often have to do with state or national laws, as has been a part of the Amish story from the very beginning. There is a growing recognition of the problem of abuse as well. The impact of tourism can also be hotly debated. Here we can clearly see that the Amish are not "cookie-cutter people." And in the end, these may end up being problems about which the church and congregation as a whole need to take a stand.

Amish and the Government

Mice in the Corn Barrel

We are aware that our forefathers did not enjoy the privileges we do today. In Anabaptist martyr days, they paid for their faith with poverty and suffering, and even with their lives. They did not fit in with what the government required of them.

The time came when many families sought relief by moving, at great sacrifice, to the United States and Canada in quest of religious liberty. Here in America, the government did not interfere with the people's right to believe as they chose. As one generation followed another, this freedom came to be almost taken for granted.

Eventually, there were again changes. Governments became more powerful and more restrictive. Income was taxed to provide funds for more government programs. Legislation was passed to allow people to pay into a government-run old-age insurance plan. It was designed to give security to people who were used to prosperity but were too old to work and care for themselves. The Plain people were not favorably impressed.

Then in the 1950s, new laws made the government's Social Security program compulsory. By law, everyone was required to take part, whether or not you were agreed with it.

The leaders of our churches pled earnestly with the government to be excused from their social programs. The issue seemed so urgent that a nationwide steering committee was formed in 1966 to represent the Plain people, monitor the laws, and resolve conflicts where possible.

As the Amish and Mennonites presented their plea for release from government social programs, they used various biblical teachings as grounds for their concerns. We work quietly to earn our living. We do not expect to live on gifts or handouts.

Second, it would be inconsistent to depend on the world for sustenance when we as Christians claim to trust in God and to be content with what he gives us by the work of our hands. To consent even to paying in would bring the temptation later to feel entitled to the benefits. Half a century later, it is not hard to see how well grounded their concerns were.

Today, many younger people see their neighbors accepting health insurance benefits from their jobs, in addition to their regular pay. There is increased pressure to accept farm subsidies. Just think how that money would help pay our mortgage!

When letters started coming from the government this past summer, offering stimulus checks, it was a little hard to know what we should make of it. I was still pondering the matter as I headed one day to a neighbor's shop to have some repairs made. While I was there, he asked, "Say, how do we look at these checks being offered to us?"

I returned the question. "How do *you* feel about them?"

"Come over here. I want to show you something," he said as he led me to a corner of his shop where he had a couple of barrels of corn to feed to his horse. One barrel had only about six inches of corn left in it. He grabbed it by the rim and shook it vigorously. He pointed, and I looked into the barrel. The thin layer of corn had come alive with mice that could not get out of the barrel.

"When this barrel was full," my neighbor said, "the mice could eat here and leave. Or they could eat anywhere else they pleased. They were free to choose their coming and going. But they grew dependent on the corn that was here. With the passing of time, they did not notice the lowering of the corn level and their shrinking avenue of escape. Now they are trapped. I control their ability to come and go. Their dependence on my corn has given me complete control of their lives."

It has been both challenging and heartening to me this past summer to discover how many people do not feel comfortable to accept questionable funds. Although it was a bit unclear whether this particular program was improper for us to accept, it was fairly clear that refusing it did not in any way violate what we profess to believe.

—David F. Yoder, Middlebury, December 2008

Moving Out

As noted previously, different scriptural interpretations or disagreements over dress, technology, or other matters within the church can result in Amish leaving for a more liberal, usually non-Amish church. The following writers reflect on the reasons for and the impact of this.

The Danger of Church Shopping

Beware of the mindset of "church shoppers." You will likely have concerned neighbors who will caution you about this danger. They will say, Once you start moving, you won't be able to stop.

Once we go about picking a church like we decide which of ten desserts on the table best suits our fancy, we have become church shoppers. Unfortunately, church shoppers rapidly become "church hoppers." They can't seem to find any church that is good enough.

But it is a different matter altogether for a church to begin, founded on the strength of others' weaknesses. When people band together mainly because they all oppose the old church, and have little unity otherwise, they have some troubled waters to cross.

And yet we know there is a time for improvement, a day for reform. It need not lead you astray. Shun division and pursue peace. Be sure your motives are clear. May you discern the difference between change for the better and change-mindedness that is never satisfied.

—Anonymous, February 2005

The Empty Pew

The steady clip-clop, clip-clop of horses' hooves striking against the hard-topped road echoed and reechoed throughout the valley. The driver of one of these buggies was a young man in his mid-twenties, whom we shall call Lloyd. He was looking forward to worshiping and fellowshiping with his friends and church brethren.

A wave of warm air greeted him as he stepped inside and found a place to sit. Soon a hymn was announced, and the service officially began. Lloyd joined in as the rich tones rose and fell in unison.

Then he noticed it. The empty pew. Automatically his thoughts went to the person who used to sit there till just a short time ago. He thought of the many times he had noticed this man—the way he had with children. You could see the love he showed them as he bent and whispered in their ears, comforting them when they were tired of sitting still, and the respect they showed him in return. He had seemed to be sincere, filling his place in the church.

But now he had left, taking his family with him. The place he had filled in the church was empty. The community of believers was no longer complete. There was a vacancy.

But the saddest part was that the Plain church had no longer been good enough for him. He had felt enlightened and removed his family to what he called a more spiritual church, accepting along with it a liberal, worldly way of life. How could something be more spiritual and more worldly at the same time? Why couldn't a person become more spiritual within the restricted shelter of the Plain church? That would help build the church instead of tearing it down.

It reminded Lloyd of a stone wall that had been standing straight and tall. But now a stone had been torn from the wall. And as the stone rolled out, it loosened many smaller stones.

The wall was still there, but it was no longer as strong. There was a big gaping hole in the middle of it.

With time, other stones would again fill the gap in the wall. Younger ones will come and the empty pew will be filled, the hurts will be healed, the rifts mended. But to some of those who were closely involved, there will always remain an empty place, a lingering pain deep in their hearts, the memory of a brother who chose to leave. For those people there will always be an empty pew.

—*An Old Order Mennonite*, August/September 2005

Problems with Abuse

What Is Abuse?

I have been thinking, what really is child abuse? The dictionary gives the definitions for abuse as (1) to use or to treat wrongly, (2) to insult. So I have given this matter some thought. Here are a few ideas which came to my mind that may help us parents define abuse.

1. It is to spank a child anywhere on the body except the well-padded "seat."

2. Abuse is to discipline when there is a lack of self-control in the one giving discipline, especially if it is in anger or exasperation.

3. It is abusive to the child to give in to his whims, or to let him harm himself without restraint or discipline.

4. It is abuse if we fail to teach them God's Word and instruct them in his way, or if we fail to be a good Christian example to our children.

5. It is abuse if we fail to praise them for a job well done.

6. It is abuse if we do not respect their feelings.
7. It is not being fair to our children if we do not give them guidance and encouragement when they face something new or difficult.
8. If we do not spend time with our children, we are depriving them of something they need very much.
9. We abuse our children if we do not provide an atmosphere of love, trust, hope, happiness, and faith in God.
—*A Parent Who Is Too Often Lax*, July 1996

Abuse Is Sin

Any abuse, whether physical, sexual, or verbal, is sin. It is totally contrary to the teachings of Jesus. A husband who abuses his wife is breaking his vow to love and cherish her as long as they live. A father who misuses his children is disobedient to the command "Bring them up in the nurture and admonition of the Lord" [Ephesians 6:4].

If a case is known to the ministry, it is their duty to investigate. They have a responsibility to the abuser to make it plain that the sin of abuse is as serious as drunkenness and adultery. Unless repentance is evident, it is needful to excommunicate the abuser so he realizes the seriousness of his position.

Often, victims of abuse feel they themselves are somehow responsible for this situation. They need to be assured that there is nothing they could possibly have done that excuses the abuser's actions. When someone is hurting physically, efforts are made so the healing process can work. This is also important for mental and emotional wounds.

—*A concerned brother*, February 2011

A Survivor's Journey

The journey away from the bondage of sexual abuse is a long and hard one. But it is worth taking. I suffered in silence for many years until I dared to ask for help. Breaking the silence is very hard, but oh so necessary. If the abuser is a person from your church, he should be confronted by the church leaders. A female victim is not responsible to confront her abuser. One thing I finally grasped is that I need not stay a victim, but instead I can be a survivor of abuse. We need help in sorting out and dealing with our past before we can grow or heal spiritually. No matter how much the abuser threatens you into silence, you have the responsibility to bring dark things to the light.

—*No name, please*, April 2007

Facing the Truth

I am a teenage girl, and my heart goes out to children who are in an abusive home. I have never experienced any outward physical abuse such as getting hit, kicked, or so on. But we children have received many inward knocks of discouragement, deceit, and confusion.

Instead of facing up to the truth, I was trying to avoid it. After such a long period of confused thoughts, God has graciously shown me the solution—to accept the truth, even if it is not a pleasant truth. I have decided to take one day at a time and leave the future in his almighty hand.

A Plea for Dad

My love goes out to you, my dad,
    For I am thinking of you tonight.
If only there were something I could do
    To help you see the light.

My heart is aching, bleeding, crushed.
    My love for you is strong.
If I have failed to do my part,
    Forgive me for this wrong.

> I'm praying for you and hoping, too,
>> That someday you can find,
> The path to happiness and truth,
>> And wondrous peace of mind.

—Seeking God's Will, July 1996

Blocked Too Long

I did not realize what I was doing to myself and my family. I did not realize that this all stemmed from the abuse I endured as a child.

With the gentle, persistent prodding of my caring husband (the only one I had confided in), I was finally convinced to search for help to work this through. Before that time, I had known of only one escape—if something reminded me, block it out, forget it, stuff it away down inside, let no one ever see it. In reality, I myself did not want to see it or think about it.

Fearfully and tremblingly, we found someone to help us work through this, and I discovered there is another way to look at it. I also discovered I had lots of bottled-up feelings from things that had happened between the ages of five and eleven. I had erected huge barriers between myself and others, and worst of all, between myself and God.

Slowly these things have turned into stepping-stones in our lives. We have been brought closer to our children. It has greatly increased our faith. I have found the healing a slow process, and when times become hard, I like to look up and think of God looking down on us and helping us along. With continued prayer and the gentle, patient help of my husband, there is a very real light at the end of the long dark tunnel.

—No Name or State, Please, February 2000

Tourism and Marketing

A City on a Hill

The Plain people have been in this country almost three hundred years, and have built up the scenic farmsteads and villages by the sweat of their collective brow. They weren't really trying to be picturesque—it just turned out that way! People came from far and wide to visit Amish country to take a little peek through a window into America's past. The question that bothers me is this: Whose values are being absorbed by whom?

While the same forces are at play in Amish communities all across the country, I will use for an example the first and most famous Amish tourist industry in the country. In Lancaster County, tourism has reached gigantic proportions. The visitors bureau, representing over five hundred attractions and businesses, spends $3 million per year getting the tourists to come.

And come they do. The flood has reached about nine million tourists a year, and they spend over $2 billion while they are there. Lancaster County, long known as the "Garden Spot of America," is blessed with over five thousand highly productive family farms, which sell about $800 million worth of farm products each year.

Oftentimes local laws are passed by savvy newcomers and their businessman allies for the "protection" of the area, assuring that the development of the area is controlled by at least somebody. And maybe not in ways that really work for the farm population. Smelly cows become an affront to sophisticated nostrils, and sweaty horses are viewed as inhumane. The residents of the area are no longer viewed as being so quaint, but rather as being backward, stupid, and a traffic hazard. The clash is on!

What really are the wishes of the community? Are they the wishes of the farmers who, though low in numbers, were there first and actually control the vast majority of the land? Or the wishes of the numerically superior town residents and professionals and businessmen, to whom development means profit? Or is it the wishes of those from other areas of the state or nation who want to see our area either developed or preserved, according to their own agenda?

Today we are no longer a despised people. We are no longer an ignored people. The world wants to be our friend, to praise us and applaud us. We have to endure countless scientific studies, doctoral dissertations, presidential visits, and TV documentaries.

What does it do to us? Well, for one thing it makes us proud of ourselves, for we are only human. The prosperity that comes along with the tourists and developers lures us away from the simple life, and from a dependence and reliance on our brother, whom we cherish.

Are we a national treasure? Will changes within our communities be a loss to society? Do we have a right to be preserved? The answer to all these questions is no. It is no because we are not a remnant from days gone by. We are a church, a living community of faith.

But of course, life actually isn't so simple. A great many of the people who come to visit would seriously want to share our faith and values. Faith is not destination, just as life is not a destination. It is a journey. Some of the people who come to visit us are on that journey of faith. Many are just starting out and may not know where they are on it, or even that they are on it at all. What they observe and learn from their visit may affect the course of their lives. Some may decide to come back later to join us. Some may take some aspect of it and use it to strengthen their own families or communities.

[As one Amish person has written,] "If you admire our faith, strengthen yours. If you admire our sense of commitment, deepen yours. If you admire our community spirit, build your community. If you admire our simple life, cut back. If you admire quality merchandise, then produce quality. If you admire deep character and enduring values, live them!"

It is easy to get the equation upside down, and to think that we are what we are because of the way we live, instead of that we live as we do because of who we are. It comes from the inside out, not from the outside in. And be sure to give the honor to the One to whom it belongs!

—Robert Alexander, October 2020

Marketing the Amish

The Amish "mystique," which has developed over the past thirty years, is the result of a number of factors. One of the most obvious is that the general society has changed so rapidly and become so modern that a horse-and-buggy society typifies to people their lost past.

The mystique, however, is more complex than that. It also involves virtues such as honesty and marital faithfulness, both stressed in Amish society but seriously compromised in the larger society. Amish craftsmanship is admired and purchased.

Advertising agencies, corporate executives, and independent retailers are fully aware of the new mystique and are using the term "Amish" to sell a great variety of products. To the customer, "Amish" is supposed to mean "well made, durable, better, dependable," and any other qualities a customer is looking for in a product. Some of the items being advertised as "Amish" are actually made by the Amish, but many are not. Let's take a look at some of the "Amish" items that have appeared in the marketplace.

Some companies do not actually use the word "Amish" in their advertisements, but include an Amish horse-and-buggy scene. This is called advertising by association. The buyer gets a mental impression that the product has "Amish quality."

A most unusual use of the Amish by association in advertising appeared in the June 1992 issue of *Windows Magazine*. That periodical does not deal with house windows but "windows" in computers. The advertisement by Amish Software, Inc., of Palo Alto, California, shows a cute little "Nebraska Amish" boy and his terrier. There is absolutely no reason for the Amish to be associated with computer software, except for customer appeal. For those of us not familiar with computer programming, the terms used in the advertisement are meaningless: Amish Launch, Amish Desk, Amish File, Amish Memopad, and Amish Clock. But the software company obviously thought their product needed something to help it sell, so they chose the Amish.

Then there is the term "Amish Country," where the advertiser is not saying the Amish actually made the item, but that it was produced in an area where they reside. The implication is that items made in "Amish Country" are quality products, more dependable and reliable. In Ohio, there are Amish Country Potato Chips and a host of other products: cheese, meat, and furniture. In York, Pennsylvania, there is a company called Amish Country Spas.

Then, of course, "Amish" chickens and turkeys are regularly advertised. What about "Amish" sheep? The following appeared in a Smicksburg, Pennsylvania, letter published in the November 4, 1992, issue of *Die Botschaft*:

> I had a lady in the shop last week that wanted a piece of sheep skin, and I was asked if it was Amish sheepskin. I said, "I don't think so, and it probably wasn't a Republican or a Democrat either!" She paid for the sheepskin and gave me an awful look when she went out the door.

The problem with so many products being labeled or advertised as "Amish" is that human beings are being idealized, romanticized, and set on a pedestal where no people belong. Sooner or later customers are going to read about some Amish moral failure or obtain an inferior "Amish" product and be very disappointed in a group which professes to be devout Christians.

—David Luthy, January 1994

Plain Pride

There is a "letter" that came to us. If nothing else, it should cause people to do some deep thinking. The letter follows below . . .

Congratulations! It's hard to believe that Pathway is already thirty-four years old. How well I remember the humility of those magazines in those first years. In those days Pathway was trying to promote a deeper appreciation of our heritage. Today, it seems at times as if some writers are promoting a deeper appreciation of our superiority.

The superiority of our way of life compared to others; the superiority of our church compared to other churches; the superiority of our language; the superiority of our hymns, our tunes, our preaching; the superiority of our means of transportation; the superiority of our farming methods; the superiority of our child-rearing principles.

This "Plain pride" is also being fostered by tourism. (If people all over the world think we're so great, we really must be something.) "Plain pride" can be seen wherever there are Plain people. It is evident in the man in the carriage on the highway with a long string of cars behind him. He's probably a successful businessman or a prosperous farmer, and he got that way because he's thrifty and hardworking. He pays more taxes than most of the people in the cars behind him. Why should he bump along on the shoulder? He has as much right to the road as anyone else.

"Plain pride" is also being fostered by our government. We're bringing in the tourist dollars, so they are bending over backward to please us. Amish men are fighting the township zoning laws to enlarge their woodworking shops, and the supervisors are changing the bylaws to please them.

We are rich and increased with goods and in need of nothing. Oh, please, let us be careful! We are being blinded and enslaved by something that on the surface seems good to us. Our enemy is tricky. Let us repent and weep and pray to be rid of this "Plain pride."

—Anonymous, October 2002

THIRTEEN

People of Peace

WE HAVE ALREADY NOTED that the Amish are nonresistant and have suffered persecution, torture, and death in their history. However, for me it has also been profoundly moving to see how this commitment to nonviolence has played out in matters of war—how individuals have responded when put to the test. In the past twenty-five or so years some new stories have emerged. I include these along with some thoughts on the increase in violence in American culture, September 11, and the concept of "another kingdom."

Amish and the Civil War

This was the American Amish's fourth encounter with war: French and Indian War (1754–63), Revolutionary War (1775–83), War of 1812 (1812–15), and now the Civil War. Practically speaking, no Amish lived in the South during the Civil War. During the war's first year there was no universal conscription, the Union Army being made up entirely of volunteers. Since the Amish were conscientious objectors and did not readily enlist, they were criticized by some of their neighbors. In an attempt to explain the Amish position to the public, an anonymous Ohio writer (who merely signed his name as "S") wrote a treatise which was published early in 1862 in the *Holmes County Farmer*.

> We (the Amish or Mennonites) are religiously opposed to all wars or fighting of whatever kind or nature, believing that the Gospel forbids us to take the sword in any case whatever . . .
>
> The reader will hereby see that we regard it to be a religious duty to be obedient unto the Government under which we live, in everything that is not contrary to the Gospel, but to meet an enemy with the sword we cannot conscientiously do, believing that the Gospel teaches us otherwise. Whatever the government may demand of us in money will be carefully and honestly paid, and it is our sincere prayer that a kind Providence may so lead the destiny of our country that peace be speedily restored and that we may continue to enjoy the liberties and freedom of conscience we have so long enjoyed under our excellent Government, and that it may continue to be an asylum for those that flee from the tyranny and oppression of the old country. —S.

There was no draft until 1862, the second year of the war, and it was administered by the various states. It was not until an act of Congress was passed on March 3, 1863, that conscription was placed under the jurisdiction of the federal government. No specific exemption was made for conscientious objectors, but provisions were made to exempt any man who either "furnished an acceptable substitute to take his place in the draft" or who paid a sum "not exceeding $300" to the government "for the procuration of such substitute."

People learned of the exemption in various ways, but few as dramatically as these three Amish young men in Holmes County, Ohio. The incident is related by the grandson of one of the draftees:

On a Sunday in church there were three young men that were drafted to go to camp the following Monday morning. The members could hardly sing, so troubled were they that these young men had to go to camp with the soldiers.

Before the church meeting was over, three officers in uniform knocked at the door. Everybody expected they came to take the boys along; but the officers told them that there are men who enlisted to go in the army for the sum of $300. And if they could pay that by Monday morning, they could stay at home.

That night the church sent men from house to house; those who had money gave it. By Monday morning the $900 (a huge sum at that time) was paid, and the boys could stay at home. One of them was my grandfather. —H. A. Hershberger

Many conscientious objectors—Quaker, Dunkard, Mennonite, or Amish—debated whether it was consistent with their non-resistant faith to hire substitutes or to pay the government to hire them. Undoubtedly their opposition to that practice influenced the federal government to revise the draft law.

The new law was enacted on February 24, 1864, and specifically exempted conscientious objectors, giving them three alternatives to military service: (1) assignment to duty in hospitals; (2) assignment to the care of freedmen; (3) payment of $300 to be applied to the benefit of the sick and wounded soldiers.

No record has been found of any Amish performing either the first or second alternatives offered in the act, but various examples are known where the commutation fee of $300 was paid. One record states that the Amish congregation in Garrett County, Maryland, and Somerset County, Pennsylvania, "raised the sum of $16,000 to pay these taxes for their members who were called in the draft." That sum divided by $300 means fifty-three young men were exempted.

When the Civil War began, Christian Esch was residing in Howard County, Indiana, where an Amish settlement had existed less than two decades. Three of his sons are said to have avoided serving in the army by hiding out:

> Three of his sons—Daniel, Christian Jr., and Noah—were drafted. Since it was against their belief to go to war, these boys left word with their father to place a basket of food at a stated place every evening, and made their escape to some hiding place. The father left food for them regularly and in this way their whereabouts were unknown until the danger ceased.

In Holmes County, Ohio, three of Yost and Anna (Hochstetler) Yoder's sons enlisted. Two of them, Moses and Jacob, died during the war. Their oldest brother Noah was badly wounded but survived the war and became a doctor at Shanesville, Ohio.

Also in Holmes County, three of Jeptha T. Miller's sons joined the army; two of them, Tobias and Stephen, were killed the same day on July 10, 1863. Their brother Isaac served as an aide to General Grant and is said to be the young man with the thin mustache standing in the background in photos of General Grant and General Lee sitting at a small table during Lee's surrender at Appomattox. Isaac survived the war and owned a general store at Charm, Ohio, where he served as postmaster.

—David Luthy, March 1996

The Man Who Would Not Shoot

Christian and Daniel Good, two young Mennonites of Harrisonburg, Virginia, were drafted into the Confederate Army against their will. They were the sons of a widow, and had been almost the sole means of support for their mother and younger brothers and sisters.

Their appeals for release were ignored by officials. The two men were sent to a military camp where they remained during the winter of 1861–62. Daniel managed to slip away from the camp and attempted fleeing to the north with a group of others. But he was captured and sent to prison.

Christian, however, remained at the military camp. As the war escalated, he found himself out on the firing line. When the officer in charge gave the order to shoot at the enemy, Christian refused. He was called to appear before an officer for questioning.

"Did you shoot when you were ordered to do so?" demanded the officer.

Christian's reply was "No, I didn't see anything to shoot at."

"Didn't you see all those Yankees over there?" the officer pressed him.

"But they are *people*," Christian explained. "We don't shoot people."

The officer threatened to have Christian court-martialed and shot to death if he refused again. Christian remained true to his faith, and soon had the nickname among the other soldiers as "the man who would not shoot."

When he was questioned again, he firmly replied that he would never fire a gun at his fellow man, no matter if it cost him his life. He explained that he had a widowed mother at home who expected him to keep his sacred pledge never to fire a gun at another person. Christian Good and a number of other conscientious objectors were then assigned to drive teams of horses.

—Anonymous, January 2011

* * *

World War I: From Persecution to Acclaim

What did World War I do to our churches? In the Civil War draft, the Plain people could pay a $300 bounty and be free, but now in 1917 it was different. Our young men were being sent to army camps where they had to take a stand for their faith.

Secretary of War Newton D. Baker had sent orders to the army camps that conscientious objectors were to be treated in a humane way. But it was up to the commanders of each camp to decide what was humane. It was the army's job to train soldiers, not to coddle a bunch of German-speaking farm boys.

Some camps used extreme measures to compel these boys to wear a military uniform and to drill with the other soldiers. Rudy Yoder of near Charm, Ohio, was drafted and sent to an army camp. He refused to wear the uniform. After weeks of verbal abuse they tricked him into taking off his clothes, put them in a box, and sent them to his Ohio home. With no clothes to wear, Rudy had no choice but to wear a uniform.

When the box of clothes arrived at the home of his parents, the Jonas Yoders, they did not know what to do. Jonas went to see his friend Moses Beachey, of Farmerstown, Ohio. The men decided to travel to the army camp where Rudy was stationed. When they arrived at the camp, they asked to see the commander. They set the box of clothes in front of the commander and told him, "Secretary of War Baker said that the COs should be treated in a humane way. If you don't give Rudy his Amish clothes back today, we will send a telegram to Secretary Baker." Thereupon, they gave the clothes back to Rudy.

The tourists flock to our communities. Amish food, Amish quilts, Amish this, Amish that. It is popular to be Amish. But these incidents from the past tell us that this was not always so. Someday it may once again not be so popular to be Amish.
—Monroe L. Beachey, March 1994

* * *

The Increase of Violence

Recently I had the opportunity to read a thought-provoking article, "We Are Training Our Kids to Kill," by Lt. Col. Dave Grossman, which appeared in the July–August *Saturday Evening Post.* Grossman makes the point that killing is unnatural, and that we are all born with a powerful God-given aversion to the killing of our own kind.

During World War II, the army had a team do research on what the soldiers actually did in battle. They discovered that only about one in five could bring themselves to fire at an exposed enemy soldier. On the basis of such findings, an effort was made to desensitize the soldiers so they would be willing to kill. By the time of the Korean War about 55 percent of the soldiers were able to shoot to kill. By the Vietnam War the rate had risen to 90 percent. Grossman ought to know because it was formerly his job to train soldiers to shoot to kill.

He asserts that the same kind of desensitizing is happening to children who are exposed to television, movies, and video games. Grossman is convinced the accelerated murder rate is worldwide and is because of TV and movies presenting violence to children. [He writes,] "We have raised a generation of barbarians who have learned to associate violence with pleasure, like the Romans cheering and snacking as the Christians were slaughtered in the Colosseum."

Meanwhile, video games are the newest big-time contributor to the wave of violence in our land. The two young men who were responsible for the school massacre at Littleton, Colorado, and then took their own lives spent hours upon hours playing the game *Doom*, in which participants see who can rack up the most kills. All this time they are learning to point and shoot with deadly accuracy.

Surely a world that is increasingly filled with violence has nothing to offer us.

—David Wagler, August/September 1999

* * *

Citizens of Another Kingdom

The ordeal that shook our nation on September 11, 2001, has spawned many news stories and public debate. Now that the first anniversary of the event is here, perhaps we should take time to review how we as nonresistant and non-violent Christians should respond in such times of national emergency.

First of all, we ought to avoid any show of patriotism. As Christians, should we feel more horrified at the loss of five thousand lives in these terrorist attacks than we are at the many thousands of refugees in Bosnia who have died of starvation, or the orphans of Liberia, or the martyrdom of Chinese Christians? We need to work at keeping our feelings neutral for all killings and all wars. All are precious in God's sight. That is why we cannot show patriotism, or fly our country's flag.

Does that mean we should turn against our country and roundly criticize our government? It is so easy to be drawn into government-bashing when others around us are openly critical or even scornful of federal policies. Such disrespect does not belong to our Christian witness. Rather, we need to be entirely neutral on these issues.

We are to be respectful of our government, pay our taxes, pray for [our leaders], and be obedient in all things that are not contrary to God's will. We can still respect our country and thank God for the privileges we still enjoy under its government. Yet we need to keep in mind that our citizenship is not on this earth, but in heaven.

So if our American neighbor asks us where we stand, we should clearly explain it. He may not agree with us, but he will likely appreciate it if we take the time to explain that in these earthly affairs we choose to be neutral and uninvolved. But when it comes to the affairs of God's kingdom, we wish to take a firm stand for what is right.

—*A Wisconsin husband, with the help of his wife*, October 2002

FOURTEEN

Amish Humor

IF THERE IS ONE THING that I like to remind readers of, it is that the Amish do have a sense of humor. When I talk to Amish people I know, it often doesn't take long to hear a funny comment or a chuckle. But this is usually gentle humor, not derisive, sarcastic, or unkind. In *Family Life*, I often found this humor best revealed in poems—something else the average reader may be surprised to see. (One rarely sees poetry cited in academic books on the Amish.) Particularly at stressful moments in daily life, laughter often really is "the best medicine."

Wraparound Riddle

I flap it at the chickens
when they get into my garden;
I twist it in my fingers
when I beg somebody's pardon.
It can wipe a dusty table;
it can wipe a drippy nose;

224

And I never have to hunt it—
    where I go, it always goes.

It has sheltered bashful children,
    it has steadied little feet;
When I wrap it round a handle,
    it protects me from the heat.
It has toted beans and carrots,
    it has cradled baby pigs,
It is loaded in October
    with the 'taters Hubby digs.

Have you all found out the riddle?
    —For the few who cannot guess,
It's the multipurpose apron
    that I wear upon my dress!

—Janice Etter, October 1995

Dust Bunnies

The light is out, my prayers are said;
I hear a noise beneath the bed.
And so I pull my legs up tight
And yell for Mom to bring the light.
But there was nothing there at all
Except a dirty sock and ball.
"Oh my," Mom said, "dust bunnies, too.
I see I have a job to do."
And then she left and closed the door.
But I'm not frightened anymore,
And I can sleep without a light—
It's rabbits that I hear at night.

—Sharon Stoll, August/September 2017

Old Age?

The wind blew mournfully through the gnarled old willow tree, matching the feelings of the lone figure huddled beneath it and ruffling his wispy hair.

As the gloomy chap reflected on his past, he grew steadily moodier. Why had life been so cruel to him? It wasn't fair! Even his family seemed to be against him. They acted as though they didn't trust him.

At mealtimes, they hovered over him, cutting and mashing and chopping his food. If he wasn't careful how he ate, they tied a bib on him. And they spoke to him in short, simple sentences as though perhaps he couldn't understand them if they talked like normal people.

The very worst of all was how he wasn't allowed any freedom whatsoever. He couldn't go anywhere by himself. Other times, they took him places he didn't want to go. Like the time they had secretly taken him to the doctor and he didn't realize it till they were there. That time he had been very upset and didn't hesitate to let them all know it.

Suddenly his eyes brightened. Tomorrow his family would all be together. They would have to listen to him. After all, it was his birthday they would be celebrating. Surely they would respect someone of his age. Because tomorrow he would be two!

—M. K. S., February 2016

Kitchen Revolution

> Now I have to change my cooking,
> Hard as that may be.
> Hubby's test showed high cholesterol,
> Now it's up to me.

Only meat in leaner portions,
Whole wheat bread and pie,
Applesauce instead of oil,
Cook instead of fry.

You young cooks with fancy dishes,
I am warning you—
Cut the fats before your man
Has high cholesterol, too!
                    —Anonymous, February 2009

Over the years, more than fourteen hundred poems from just fourteen prolific authors have been submitted to the magazine. In 2003, readers were asked to vote for their favorite poems out of thirty-two that were submitted by these "most faithful poets." This is a shortened version of the one that received the most reader votes.

That Rooster

We have a little chicken house
That's filled with nests and things,
And in it are a dozen hens
With brown and shining wings.
A rooster! Yes, a rooster, too,
To scratch about and peck,
But if he wasn't there at all
I'd be still happier yet.

One day I went to fetch the eggs
Without a wary thought,
And all the hens came running in
To see what I had brought,
When all at once the atmosphere

Erupted fearfully—
A flapping, slapping, angry thing
Came bursting into me.

I knew it was that rooster
And it made me sort of mad;
He scratched me and he whacked me
And he tried to hurt me bad;
And when he left, I hurried from
The scene where we had fought,
Then stuck my face across the gate
And told him what I thought:
So animals are nice to have—
Of that there is no doubt;
But roosters in the farmyard
Are what I can do without.

—Anonymous, July 2003

Sharing the Baby

We just got a new baby brother;
God sent us this special surprise.
He came in the wee hours of morning
Before we had opened our eyes.
And then when we finally got him,
We thought we would hold him a lot,
For we are his two bigger sisters,
And fill a most singular spot.
Guess what . . . !

Our dad likes to hold him,
For this is his very first son.
And Mom needs to have him most often
To rock him, for she is the one

Who feeds him whenever he's hungry,
And burps him each time he is done.

Our uncles and aunts bring our cousins;
Our grandpas and grandmas come, too,
And friends come by sixes and dozens,
Until there is nothing to do
But patiently, wishfully watch them,
Till everyone's visits are through.
    The next time God sends us a baby,
    We are going to ask him for two!
                    —L. J. Martin, February 2014

The following was written in response to an article, "Plain Is Not Fancy," about using faddish names rather than "Plain" or biblical ones. It makes fun of the way the Amish often identify people with the same name by using a nickname or a family relation.

Who?

Sadie walked to the mailbox to get the mail. As she headed back to the house, her neighbor Leah came out her driveway. "Hi, Sadie, did you hear that Moses have a baby boy?"

"Mose who?" asked Sadie.

"Oh, you know, Jake Zook's Jake's Mose.

"Oh, yes, and what's the baby's name?" wondered Sadie.

"Why, they named him Jake," answered Leah.

"That's nice!" Sadie exclaimed. "But who is Mose's wife?"

"Butter Mary's Butter and Lizzie's Katie," explained Leah.

Would there not be just a few more ordinary names which could be used? Isn't this other extreme quite real in many large communities? Sign me,

        —*Wild Harry's M. E.'s E. B.'s Daniel*, April 2001

Soup Song

Oh soup, good soup!
Tantalize-your-nose soup,
Warm-you-to-your-toes soup,
Wise-the-cook-that-chose soup.
   Try some soup tonight.

Stock soup, stew soup,
Old-and-tried-and-true soup,
Search-for-something-new soup.
   What variety!

Red soup, green soup,
Fill-a-hungry-teen soup,
Try-a-hearty-bean soup,
Sodium low or lean soup,
   Meeting varied needs.

Yum soup, yam soup,
Oyster, fish, or clam soup.
Cheesy chowder, ham soup,
Eat-with-bread-and-jam soup.
Comfort food for all.
   —Mrs. Andrew N. Miller, December 2010

Milkin' Time

Red cows, black cows,
White-strip-down-the-back cows.
"Nothing do you lack, cows,
On my dairy farm."

"Hey, cows! Ho, cows!
You must get up and go, cows.

Why are you so slow, cows,
When it's milking time?"

Good cows, poor cows;
"Come in the stable door, cows;
Watch the slippery floor, cows—
Take your time in here."

First cows, last cows,
Very slow and fast cows.
"Milking time is past, cows,
You did well tonight."

—Anonymous, February 2012

Of Houses and Homes

Darling house, dream house,
Cutest little cream house,
Beside-the-splashing-stream house,
  Just for you and me
  NOW . . .
Tattered house, battered house,
Floors-are-stained-and-splattered house,
Youthful-dreams-are-shattered house
  By reality.
  BUT . . .
Girls' home, boys' home,
Strewn-about-with-toys home,
Filled-with-happy-noise home,
  Happy family!
Caring home, sharing home,
Others'-burdens-bearing home,
For-heaven-we're-preparing home,
  Blessed eternity!

—Mrs. N. M., April 2018

FIFTEEN

Odds and Ends

READING THROUGH THE PAST twenty-five years of monthly magazines, I sometimes came across items that simply did not fit into one of my preordained chapter titles. Yet I didn't want to lose them. And so, as with the first volume, here is a chapter where you never know what you will read next.

Applesauce Day

Preserving foods in jars (canning) is common among the Amish. Visitors are often amazed at the hundreds of jars found in some homes, prepared in the summer or fall to enjoy over the winter and coming months. Making applesauce has always been popular. This article provides a delightful look at what a day of canning is like.

When my husband comes in for breakfast, he is carrying the apple cutter, a gadget that swiftly cuts up a bushel of apples as the long handle moves up and down, forcing the apple through the eight-piece wedged cutter blades.

After breakfast and devotions are past, we clear both kitchen tables. Dad goes to the basement for empty jars, while Mom gets the water running to first wash the dishes, and then the jars. When the jars are clean, they are set in rows on the white sheet.

On the older, everyday table, Dad has set a box of apples and the cutter, for that is usually his job. Now to get some clean water into the sink tub to wash the "schnitz"—the peeled and sliced apples—and to fill kettles to place on the woodstove, which is firing away. Dad gets the Victorio strainer from the pantry and assembles it, fastening it to the table beside the jars.

Before long we have the first large bowls on the kitchen chair filling up with steaming applesauce, ready to be ladled into jars. A 500-mg vitamin C tablet is dropped into the top of each full quart jar to keep the sauce from turning dark once it is canned. The lids are screwed on, and the full jars are ready to be processed in the two pressure cookers on the gas range. The two quarts of water in each cooker are partly hot by now.

The cooker lids are fastened as for pressure canning, but the vent is left open during the whole process. Once it is steaming full blow, the timer is set for fifteen minutes. Then the burner is turned off and let set for five minutes more before loosening the lid and removing the jars.

In a spare moment, Mom scrubs a few potatoes for dinner and pops them into the oven, since it is good and hot anyhow.

But finally the last apples are cooking, and a few leftovers warmed up, along with applesauce, of course, and dinner is ready to be eaten.

Well! There is still time to go ahead and put the Jonathan apples through for apple butter. So Dad sorts out a half bushel and puts them through, to which ten cups of sugar (brown and white), two cups vinegar, three pints orange juice, one pint elderberry juice, and one teaspoon salt are added.

234 / AMISH VOICES

Evening comes and after counting ninety-three quarts of applesauce and eighteen pints of apple butter, everyone is ready to take off their splattered clothes and go for a good warm bath. Tired but happy, they are then ready to retire for the night. It has been a rewarding day for all.

—*A homemaker*, October 2004

Brain Teasers

There are usually brain teasers or some kind of word quiz in every issue of *Family Life*, so I thought it would be fun to include a few here. Answers are at the end of this chapter.

Nine Busy Neighbors
Using the following clues, see if you can fill in the chart below.
1. The Albrechts live in a green house.
2. The man in the red house is forty years old.
3. The eight Ebersol children enjoy riding their horse, Rosie.
4. Luke Troyer is three years younger than the teacher.
5. Raymond Brubacher, the teacher, is thirty-six years old and lives in a brick house with his wife Ruthann.
6. Forty-three-year-old Mark and his family live in a stone house.
7. Laverne is forty-eight.
8. The family with nine children owns a dairy farm.
9. Ruthann goes shopping with their frisky young horse, Judy.
10. The Martins live in a white house.
11. Mark Snyder is the community carpenter.
12. Timothy and Laura Martin's three children enjoy

feeding their tame horse, May.

13. Murray Albrecht is seventeen years younger than Laverne Ebersol.

14. Lloyd's faithful Lady helps take baked goods to the farmers' market every Saturday.

15. Willard and Alma Zehr live in a new yellow house.

16. Karen Ebersol is the welder's wife.

17. Luke has seven children.

18. The five Albrecht boys like helping their mother in the fabric store.

19. Carl is forty years old.

20. Alma Zehr takes her children to school each day with Jewel.

21. Carl Kuepfer, the hog farmer, likes his horse Star.

22. The butcher lives in a brown house.

23. Shirley Albrecht is the mother of five robust boys.

24. Lloyd and Dorothy Wengerd live in a blue house and are kept busy with four children and a bakery.

25. The ten Snyder children enjoy helping their father in his carpentry shop.

26. The Ebersol family is pleased with their new gray house.

27. Elsie Kuepfer takes her six children to town with faithful old Star.

28. Murray likes when Rocket trots swiftly.

29. Marlene Troyer, the butcher's wife, is nervous about taking her seven children to school with new horse Dusty.

30. The baker is twenty-nine years old.

31. Willard Zehr is ten years older than Carl Kuepfer.

32. Twenty-seven-year-old Timothy enjoys his work as a blacksmith.

33. Raymond has no children to greet when he comes home from his job.

34. Mark's wife Rosemarie enjoys driving Prince.

First name	Age	Wife's name	Last name	Occupa-tion	Horse's name	No. of children	Color of house

—June 2016

Scrambled States

These phrases do not make much sense, but if you unscramble the letters, they will spell names of states of the United States. See how many of them you can get before you look at the answers.

1. Worn key
2. Set ax
3. Not washing
4. I fail a corn
5. Hand or slide
6. Dial for
7. Prime new hash
8. Wear lead
9. Not a man
10. Sly van in a pen
11. I cut connect
12. Coal door
13. Gone or
14. I miss our
15. Beaks ran
16. Ouch, star a lion

—September 1996

A Word Puzzle

Place the three missing letters on the line to finish the first word and start the second. The first one has been done for you.

1. Eleph **a n t** elope (elephant, antelope)
2. Dolp__ __ __ges
3. Spl__ __ __erest

4. Lea__ __ __sel
5. To__ __ __lest
6. Bigg__ __ __imate
7. Ch__ __ __plane
8. To__ __ __come
9. Tigh__ __ __der
10. Pump__ __ __dred
11. Child__ __ __ew
12. Blan__ __ __chup
13. Sylla__ __ __ssed
14. Traf__ __ __tion
15. Inter__ __ __ley
16. Mor__ __ __nish
17. Des__ __ __ite
18. Ref__ __ __egal
19. Sel__ __ __estic
20. Obli__ __ __stion

—September 1996

* * *

"Rhyming" Aaron Beiler

It would be impossible to mention all the memorable people who have borne the Beiler/Byler surname. One, though, is so unusual and should be mentioned—"Rhyming" Aaron L. Beiler, who was born May 9, 1881. It is not known at what age he began conversing in rhymes. The story goes that one of the ministers was sent to ask him about his unusual habit and whether a person should talk that way. Aaron is said to have replied in rhyme: "Ich ub mich net drinn / es kommt just im Sinn / woever ich bin." Translated into English, it loses its rhyming effect: "I don't practice; it just comes to mind wherever I am."

—David Luthy, May 1995

A Homemade Butter Churn

I took an old Maytag agitator that was chipped but in good shape otherwise. Then I bolted four gallon tin cans, one in each corner of the agitator. I also bolted them together where the cans joined each other at the top.

Next I took a wire around the four tins. Now we simply drop a plastic Skippy peanut butter jar into each of the tins, after filling them from one-half to three-fourths full of cream, and start the washing machine and let it agitate until the butter has formed. If the cream is thick and the right temperature, you should have butter within fifteen to twenty minutes.

—Daniel Borntreger, July 2002

Use a large, sturdy pillowcase to wash carrots, small cucumbers, potatoes, and other vegetables in your washer. This makes them nice and clean, and you need only rinse and trim them. Vary the washing time as to how firm your vegetables are.

—Anonymous, August/September 2009

My Favorite Store

Oh, come with me early this morning
  For our food supply is low,
And I know a place that is open
  Whenever we care to go.

The displays of produce are lovely,
  Some corn on the ear we'll choose,
And such red, juicy tomatoes.
  How could we ever refuse?

A few late black raspberries—
    There are just enough for pie.
It's nearly time for us to leave
    For our "cart" is piled up high.

We'll stop yet at the florist aisle—
    What displays there are today!
Glads, phlox, and blue forget-me-nots.
    We'll choose a nice bouquet.

Now this store has no checkout—
    We may have it all for free,
For this little store's our garden
    And we've paid in work, you see.
                —Rebecca Miller, October 1998

An Unusual Marriage

From several sources, I learned of a very unusual Amish marriage in Holmes County, Ohio, shortly before 1900. At that time there were perhaps a half-dozen church districts in the area. The bishop of the Bunker Hill district was David S. Miller, often referred to as "Glay Dave."

In Bishop Miller's congregation was a widow, Katie, whose husband Christian Yoder had passed away about twenty years earlier. She and her husband had been childless, and she was now between sixty-five and seventy years old. Among her childhood acquaintances was a Daniel J. Byler, who was several years older than she.

Meanwhile, this Daniel J. Byler had moved with his family to Geauga County, Ohio. His wife died March 11, 1893, of dropsy and consumption. Daniel had been ordained as a minister, and several of his children were living in Holmes County.

As a lonesome widower, Daniel's thoughts turned to Katie, the girl he had known in his younger years. Daniel at the age of seventy was seeking a new companion. Life was not complete without a wife at his side.

Katie, or Mrs. Yoder, gave her consent, and plans soon took form. The marriage ceremony was to take place at the close of a regular Sunday church service. It would not be a full-fledged wedding, and yet the sermon that day was a wedding sermon. The gray-haired couple sat side by side, waiting to speak their wedding vows.

Unknown to anyone else in the audience, the widow Katie was doing some serious thinking. Doubts churned in her mind. Did she really wish to disrupt her comfortable life to marry this man at her side?

Shortly before it was time for the vows, the doubts got the best of Katie. She rose and left the room. Bishop Miller was about to ask the two to come forward for marriage, when he realized the bride-to-be was no longer present. How long he may have waited we do not know, but at last the services were dismissed, because Katie obviously had left for her home.

Poor, disappointed Daniel! The next day he decided to go to Bishop Miller's home to ask for counsel. When he arrived, he was told that Bishop Miller was in his blacksmith shop. So Daniel went out to the shop, and was soon pouring out his troubles.

Talk about a coincidence! The widow Katie was having second thoughts. How could she make things right? She made her way to Bishop Miller's house, and Mrs. Miller suggested she go talk to him in his blacksmith shop. When she entered, how startled she was to find that Daniel was also there.

As the bishop listened, he sensed that both Daniel and Katie regretted the way things had turned out. Bishop Miller asked Katie if she was now willing to marry Daniel, and she said she was.

According to the story that has come down through generations, he then once again reminded them of the biblical teachings on marriage, and then decided, "You have been duly published, and I have already preached the wedding sermon. If you are willing, I see no reason I can't marry you right now."

Some witnesses were summoned, and the ceremony was not long delayed. The two left the blacksmith shop as man and wife.

—J. S., August/September 2020

* * *

Answers to the quiz "Nine Busy Neighbors"

First name	Age	Wife's name	Last name	Occupation	Horse's name	No. of children	Color of house
Luke	33	Marlene	Troyer	Butcher	Dusty	7	Brown
Raymond	36	Ruthann	Brubacher	Teacher	Judy	0	Brick
Mark	43	Rosemarie	Snyder	Carpenter	Prince	10	Stone
Laverne	48	Karen	Ebersol	Welder	Rosie	8	Gray
Timothy	27	Laura	Martin	Blacksmith	May	3	White
Murray	31	Shirley	Albrecht	Fabric store owner	Rocket	5	Green
Lloyd	29	Dorothy	Wengerd	Baker	Lady	4	Blue
Willard	50	Alma	Zehr	Dairy farmer	Jewel	9	Yellow
Carl	40	Elsie	Kuepfer	Hog farmer	Star	6	Red

Answers to "Scrambled States"

1. New York 2. Texas 3. Washington 4. California 5. Rhode Island 6. Florida 7. New Hampshire 8. Delaware 9. Montana 10. Pennsylvania 11. Connecticut 12. Colorado 13. Oregon 14. Missouri 15. Nebraska 16. South Carolina

Answers to "A Word Puzzle"

1. ant 2. hin 3. int 4. ves 5. tal 6. est 7. air 8. wel 9. ten 10. kin 11. ren 12. ket 13. ble 14. fic 15. val 16. tar 17. ign 18. ill 19. dom 20. que

SIXTEEN

Amish Parables

WHEN I PUT TOGETHER the first volume of excerpts from *Family Life*, I found many stories that taught a lesson or carried a special message. These tended to be based on everyday happenings that caused the writer to reflect on a bigger idea. This, of course, reminded me of how Jesus did the same thing, getting a point across by telling a simple story. And that's how I came up with this chapter, "Amish Parables." These stories continue to be some of my favorite parts of the magazine, and I only wish there were space to include more of them. So we conclude this book with some of the best, and I hope they will inspire and touch you as much as they did me.

More Than a Shell

It was a perfect summer day, and we were enjoying a buggy ride through the idyllic countryside.

"What's that, Mom?" asked my son, pointing out the window.

"That's a graveyard."

"What's a graveyard, and what are all those stones for?"

I cringed as I answered him, "That's where they bury people who have died. Those stones have their names on them. But just their bodies are buried there."

How can we help our children understand death and resurrection when we, as adults, sometimes struggle to comprehend it? I wondered helplessly.

"When we die, our body is just an empty, useless shell. God's plan is to give us a new body that is perfect."

My son was not quite school-age yet, and the thought of being apart from me was unsettling. *Will he ever grasp this?* I wondered.

Weeks passed and summer rewarded us with the high-pitched trill of locusts. Together, we searched for empty shells on the trees. To our surprise, we found a locust just starting to crawl out of its shell. We were fascinated how he wiggled out of his cramped quarters, dried his wings, and slowly climbed upward, out of sight into the tree's foliage.

"Mom! That's what happens when someone dies, right? They climb out of their shell and go way up there and sing!"

"Exactly," I agreed. "That locust wouldn't even want his shell anymore; neither will we want or need our earthly body when we die. We will be happy, living with Jesus."

I breathed gratefully, "Thank you, Lord, for showing my son through nature what I have been trying to teach him."

—Leona Troyer, July 2020

Drive Safely

I was on my way to town, seven miles distant, but first I stopped at our neighbor's house to drop off a note. I told her, "I'm going to town. I have an appointment."

"Drive safely!" she said in a cheerful voice.

What made the words unusual, of course, was that I was driving a horse and buggy. My trusty mare is nearing her twentieth birthday, so there was certainly no danger that I would exceed the speed limit!

The more I thought of her words of caution, the more I was impressed that they were very fitting. Any time we venture onto the highway, we are at risk of an accident. The rules for driving safely apply equally well to a horse-drawn vehicle as they do to an automobile.

What really caused me to think, however, was how fitting those same words, "Drive safely!" applied to our spiritual journey through life. In the list of common sense safety rules below, I have added a spiritual application:

1. Be alert! In our spiritual lives, we need to have our eyes and ears open to every danger.

2. Obey all traffic laws. God has standards of morality and integrity that he would have us obey. To disregard God's moral laws is to invite spiritual disaster.

3. Have one's vehicle in good repair. We need to have our spiritual house in order—at peace with God, and as much as possible, at peace with our fellow men. If we live in spiritual defeat, we are due for an accident.

4. Don't exceed the speed limit. Let us take care not to be drawn "into the fast lane" of life.

5. Be visible. Our faith will not be hidden to others. Our identity with God's children will protect us from many perils of the surrounding society.

6. Be courteous. We will show respect and courtesy to others, and keep out of the way of those who are in fast lane, and not needlessly offend them.

7. Stay on the route that leads to our destination, and then back home. To stay "on course" means to stay on the narrow way of which Jesus spoke in Matthew 7:13. May God keep us in his care and enable us, by grace, to arrive at our eternal destination.

Let us make every effort to "drive safely."

—Anonymous, December 2013

Lessons from a Woodstove

I am an advocate of each set of newlyweds' acquiring a woodstove. Many good lessons can be learned from it. There is quite an art in taking care of one.

One lesson for newlyweds is to learn how to keep a fire going. We don't want to keep piling on wood and poking around at it. Before we know it, the stove is red-hot and we have too much heat, which is very hard on the stove.

Just so, an intense person will see all kinds of opportunities and will go tearing about. A red-hot worker can get a lot done, but it can be a little hard on relationships.

There is also the chance of explosions if we completely shut off an overheated stove because the wood is hot enough to give off gases, and if the drafts are completely shut there is not enough oxygen to properly burn those gases.

If we have a partner who can work up a lot of steam, and there arises a controversy, we need to be careful not to just shut them up. This could cause an explosion and is not good for our health or relationship. We need to consider the situation calmly and speak tactfully until a cooldown has been achieved.

We need two pieces of wood beside each other in the stove to keep a steady fire going. One piece burns sporadically and has a tendency to go out. We need two good-sized chunks, and they should be arranged so they will roll together as they burn. If they roll apart, they will soon die out. Leave the draft open just a crack so the fire still gets enough oxygen to keep it going for the night.

A marriage also needs two people working together, with the warmth of love burning between them, warm enough that acts of kindness radiate around them, and they need to pull in the pure oxygen of the Word.

If they are apart for very long or very often, it is just as deadly to the spark of love as it is when two pieces of wood roll apart. The fire will slowly die out and they will wake up to a cold house and cold hearts.

Two pieces of seasoned hardwood in the stove and two earnest newlywed Christians are a delightful combination. As they tend the fire in the stoves and the fire in their hearts, it has a tendency to bring them closer together. It is never too late to put in a woodstove and learn some simple yet practical lessons in getting a steady fire of love burning in our hearts.

—Anonymous, November 2016

A Key Place to Fill

Young Herman was dissatisfied. He longed to do something great for God, something of importance. Helping his father on the farm seemed like such a dull assignment. How could his life count for something if he never did anything more important than plow the fields and feed the cows, day after day? Then one day Herman chanced across an item in his reading that caused him to stop and think:

ALL MXMBXRS ARX KXY MXMBXRS

Xvxn though my typxwritxr is an old modxl, it works quitx wxll, xxcxpt for onx of the kxys. It is trux, thxrx arx forty-fivx kxys that function wxll xnough, but onx kxy makxs thx diffxrxncx.

Somxtimxs it sxxms to mx, our church is likx my typxwritxr ... Not all the kxys arx working propxrly. You may think, "Wxll, I am only onx pxrson. What I do won't makx or brxak thx church." Xvxry mxmbxr is nxxdxd. Xvxry mxmbxr is a kxy pxrson.

With those thoughts on his mind, Herman was humbled. If he were no longer here, Herman realized, his family would miss him, first of all. He would certainly be missed in the church. And he knew there were many younger ones who looked up to him and were following his example.

Perhaps his yearning for a greater role was not from God at all, but a result of personal ambition. Perhaps what he was doing was more important than he realized.

—Anonymous, May 2007

A Lesson from the Lawn Mower

The visiting minister was about to close his sermon, but wished to speak a few words especially to the children. "Always obey your parents," he advised. "The Bible tells us to honor father and mother. Sometimes disobedience brings regrets for a lifetime."

"I want to tell you about one little boy who disobeyed. He was no more than five years old, but already he liked to play with machinery and to figure out how it worked. It was a nice summer day, and he had turned the lawn mower upside down. He was spinning the wheels with his hand. And that made the reel click and clatter. Oh, it was fun!

"But then Dad came upon the scene. He warned his son, 'You must stop playing with the lawn mower. It is too dangerous. You could cut yourself.'

"Dad went back to his work, and the little boy thought to himself, 'I'll pull the lawn mower behind the barn where Dad won't see me.' He sneaked behind the barn and turned the lawn mower upside down again.

"All at once something happened. Dad heard the little boy crying at the top of his voice, and then he came running toward the house. There was blood dripping from one finger. The end of the boy's finger had been cut off.

"That little boy grew up to be a man, but he has never forgotten the lesson he learned that day. Every time he looks at his finger, he is reminded of how he disobeyed his father."

The minister paused and reached up to take off his glasses, folded them, and tucked them into his vest pocket. As he did so, several people in the audience noticed something they had not seen before. One finger on the minister's left hand was only a stub, half as long as it should have been!

The minister went on to say, "Boys and girls, I want you to remember this. You may be tempted to do something behind Dad's back, or so Mom doesn't see you. But don't forget, God sees all that you do. It is wrong to disobey. For the rest of your life you may be sorry you did not listen. I know, for I was that little boy who got his finger in the lawn mower."

—Anonymous, May 2006

Candles That Shine

A visit to a pioneer museum is educational, for it gives us a glimpse into the past. With a puzzled look, I studied a four-armed contraption with holes in it and other weird features. I asked my host what this contraption was for.

"Oh, that was used to make candles," he replied. "They fastened strings to it and then dipped those strings into molten wax, again and again. Maybe twenty-five times or more, but letting the wax dry each time between dips. This cycle was kept up until the candles had their desired thickness."

In a sense, raising children is like the making of candles. They are constantly being dipped into the environment that surrounds them.

Parents dip their child into the wax of obedience. Another time the child may need several dips of kindness and learn to get along with others. As the child grows older, he will need numerous dips of respect, starting with respect for parents. When these dips are well dried, there must be further dips of respect for the teacher at school, and then respect for the church, and respect for one another.

Children must also be dipped frequently into the wax of appreciation to learn that they have many blessings living in a land of freedom. Unfortunately, there may be times when a child is dipped into the wax of sin and then needs to be scraped clean from such contamination.

By the time children reach school age, their candles will begin to give light, according to the number of beneficial dips they have received from their parents, friends, and others.

A wax candle burns only until the wax is all gone. Our spiritual candle is different from that—it continues to burn for as long as we live. How much light our candle gives depends on whether we have immersed it in the wax of love, or in the wax of hate. It depends, too, how freely we have let ourselves be dipped in the wax of compassion.

The world about us is also eager to dip us into its ways. We may at times stumble and find ourselves covered with worldly wax. Our candle will then flicker and smoke until the consequences of our wrong behavior are properly dealt with.

When we were children, our parents and our childhood surroundings largely formed our candle. Our culture also placed many layers of wax on our candle, and continues to do so throughout life. This may cause our candle flame to shine in a distinct pattern that is different from the candles of others. It is not for us to pass judgment on the pattern of another candle.

The biggest challenge concerning my own candle is that others can see it much better than I can. My friends must at times dip my candle into the friendly reminder of Christian rebuke so that it does not give off smoke and burn their eyes.

—*A Deacon*, April 2006

In Our Footsteps

It happened on a cold winter day. There were about six inches of snow on the ground. Our lively five-year-old daughter was tagging along as I walked through the snow from the barn to the chicken house, doing winter chores. Just as we got to the chicken house, she said, "Dad, I am following in your tracks." Then I realized she had been trying hard to take steps just as big as mine so that she could walk exactly in the same footsteps that I had made.

I can't remember that I said anything at the time. But I do remember that her words went deeply to my heart. I couldn't help thinking she might be trying to follow my footsteps in other ways, too. Was my example worthy of being followed?

May God give us grace to be better examples so that those who follow will not go wrong if they walk in our footsteps.

—Anonymous, October 1997

Your Hyphen

We stood beside an open grave
    On that November day,
And as we watched in silence there,
    We heard the preacher say:
"Upon the headstones near at hand
    Two dates are clearly seen.
We'd like to think just now about
    The hyphen in between.

"The first date marks the starting point
    Of life on earthly sod.
The last date tells the place in time
    A soul was called to God.
Between the two, a hyphen marks
    The intervening years.
So small a thing, to represent
    The course each pilgrim steers!

"How long do you think yours will be—
    The hyphen on your stone?
How many days are left to you
    Before your life is flown?"
We do not know when God will call,
    And our short breath be flown,
And all our days be marked at last—
    A hyphen on a stone!

—L. B., November 2002

Reflections

I love lakes. Framed by forests or guarded by grasses, they maintain an unmitigated majesty. And oh, how they reflect the sunset!

Ponds, also, I love. More earthy than lakes they are, but so graceful in their commonness. And they, too, reflect the sunset.

Puddles are too muddy. I never appreciated them. Overflow of a clogged ground, they are scarcely dependable. They are useless. Insignificant. Bothersome.

I have, among my acquaintances, folks who remind me of a lake. So beautifully useful. I have also met "ponds." So calmly necessary. But there are many who are only "puddles." Obscure. Seemingly worthless. A tiny border and murky water. I have always judged them to have a colorless existence.

Last night, in a muddy puddle in the middle of our rutted driveway, I saw the sunset.

—S. J. Lehman, October 2004

The Compiler

BRAD IGOU was president and co-owner of Amish Experience in Lancaster County, Pennsylvania, and publisher of *Amish Country News*. Igou is past board chair of Discover Lancaster and recipient of its Lifetime Achievement Award. He also created the Amish Visit-In-Person Tour, which gives visitors the opportunity to personally meet and talk with the Amish where they live and work. During his time at Ithaca College, Igou lived with an Amish family for three months as part of an independent study. After graduation, he spent three years working in agricultural extension with the Peace Corps in Costa Rica. He then taught English in Japan for eight years before returning to Lancaster County, where he currently resides.

CPSIA information can be obtained
at www.ICGtesting.com
Printed in the USA
JSHW081249290323
39407JS00001B/18